Country Pine Furniture

Styles and Prices

Robert and Harriett Swedberg

Includes Other Native Woods

Books by Robert W. and Harriett Swedberg:

Off Your Rocker. Step by step techniques on refinishing and care of
wood, metal, marble. How to cane chairs.

Victorian Furniture Styles and Prices

Copyright© 1980 by
Robert W. and Harriett Swedberg

ISBN 0-87069-198-8
Library of Congress Catalog No. 76-58066

Photographs: By the Authors
Printing and Enlarging: Tom Luse

Edited by Mary Matz
Layout and Design by Marilyn Pardekooper

Published by

Wallace-Homestead
authoritative books on antiques & collectibles

Wallace-Homestead Book Company
1912 Grand Avenue
Des Moines, Iowa 50309

Dedication

To Bill and Nancy Geake Thurston, who introduced us to the world of antiques and opened the doorway to the countless friendships we have made through this mutual interest.

Acknowledgments

The authors sincerely thank the following individuals and dealers who freely gave of their time and knowledge to assist us in obtaining photographs and prices for this book. Thanks also to the individuals and dealers who did not wish to be listed.

Bernice Anderson
Lynn and Reuel Armstrong
Banowetz Antiques, Maquoketa, Iowa
Dolores and Bill Best
The Bin (Jeanne Lee), Morrison, Illinois
Barb and Dave Borden
Joyce and Don Cackler
Church Mouse Antiques (Marilyn Johnson), Port Byron, Illinois
Nancy and Bob Coopman
Nancy and Kent Cornish
Jack Cummins
Karen, Cody, and Adam Elvidge
Historic House, Ltd., Moline, Illinois
Anne and Karl Huntoon
Mr. and Mrs. Terry Lorenzen
Marty and Pete Mather
Ruth and Bill Mehuys
Mr. and Mrs. M.I. Mills
Janet and Paul Moen
Laura and Phillip Ollman
Virginia and Harold Peterson
Mary Rachel Antiques, Washington, Illinois
Pat and Jack Rossow
John and Karen Schlumbohm
Pat and Paul Schroeder
Cheryl Swedberg
Village Square Antiques (Glen M., Jerry, and Theresa Nance), Pocahontas, Illinois
Paula and Tim Ziegler
Betty and Eldon Zimmerman

Table of Contents

Preface: Prices 6
        Notes Regarding Pricing 6
        Definitions of Articles Pictured in this Book 6
           Country Furniture Defined 6
           Primitives Defined 6
Chapter 1:   Advocates and Adversaries of Country Collectibles 7
        Country Furniture Defined 9
        Primitives Defined 9
        Country Furniture Could Copy
        Classical Styles 11
Chapter 2:   Antiques: Facts, Fakes, and Foibles 13
        Antique Marriages Defined 13
        "Cobbled" Defined 14
        Reproductions Versus Fakes 15
        Detecting Alterations 16
        Detecting Age in Furniture 17
           Patina Defined 18
           Signs of Wear 18
           Pegs Have a Purpose 19
           Hardware Helps 19
           Preserve that Paint 22
           The Joiner's Joints 23
           Tools of Yore Help Designate Age 26
           Thick Wood of Random Widths Says Old 28
           Does Shrinkage Tell Age? 28
           Furniture Styles Help Determine Age 30
           Smell the Age 30
Chapter 3:   The Plumbing Problem 31
Chapter 4:   Kitchen Capers 46
Chapter 5:   Ladies and Gentlemen, Please Be Seated 81
        Windsor Chairs 85
        Hitchcock Chairs 90
        Shaker Furniture 91
Chapter 6:   The Bedchamber 110
        Rope Beds 110
        Jenny Lind Spool Beds 110
        Painted Furniture including Cottage Suites 112
Chapter 7:   'Bye Baby Bunting 125
Chapter 8:   Primarily Primitive 133
Other Helpful Books 142
Glossary 143
Index 149
About the Authors 152

Preface

Prices

The matter of pricing pieces in this book is a task beyond the scope of solely these writers or other writers who propose to know the dollar sign on each antique item.

Notes Regarding Pricing

In our book *Victorian Furniture, Styles and Prices,* this job was indeed easier because Victorian furniture could be classified quite definitely as sideboards, china cabinets, secretaries, lift-top commodes, et cetera, and there were thousands of such articles made to be sold. Therefore, our questionnaire which we sent to two hundred dealers throughout the country gave us our original price scale.

Now, with country, many pieces unique in themselves, pricing in this book has been done on these bases: 1. the selling tag in a dealer's shop   2. the top bid at auction   3. the value set on the piece by the owner. In essence, this was how prices were established.

Definitions of Articles Pictured in This Book

A description of articles found in this book must be considered.

Country Furniture Defined

Early country furniture was primarily utilitarian, made from necessity to fit a particular need; generally crafted at home, by hand, out of native woods in rural regions or on the frontier; and most was unadorned, often quaint, in the simplicity of its design.

Primitives Defined

Primitives are closely akin to country, the twain tending to overlap; yet, customarily primitives are the cruder, functional items from the past, the early ones hand-fashioned when a need arose, often with limited tools. Included in this class are non-furniture articles such as washing machines, wringers, or early sleds, now obsolete, but not yet quite antique by the hundred year old test, but found in current home decors. Rustic articles from stores and barns, or representative castoffs from various occupations are present also.

Generally, this book is mainly plain — pine, that which is still available to the average collector; but all native woods are given consideration when the "feel" is country.

Chapter 1
Advocates and Adversaries of Country Collectibles

Country furniture and primitives are not for everybody.

When one devotee of rural-type home decorating was a newlywed, she purchased a battered pine hog scalder in an antique shop. Enchanted and delighted with her rustic acquisition, a reminder of autumn butchering time down on the farm, she could envision it as a one-of-a-kind table in a casual setting. Her visiting eight-year-old niece, while seemingly sharing her aunt's enthrallment with the outcast, later confessed to her mother, "I feel *so* sorry for Auntie. She's too poor to buy good furniture, but I pretended her table was neat because she was excited about it."

In one family, a bride heard these consoling words, "They'll do until you can afford something better," from a sympathetic visitor who inspected the younger woman's prized heritage heirloom rush seated chairs from the early 1800s, by her tastes, finding them deficient.

Another couple acquired a hard-to-discover, slightly sway-back vintage pine harvest table. They were asked, "Does it have a formica top?" (Well, hardly!) One unimpressed friend offered a choice of services. For a mere $5.00, he'd haul it away, but for ten, he'd burn it.

Hog scalder, pine, 1¹/₈″ to 1¼″ thick, large square nails. Size: 52″ wide, 24″ deep, 17½″ high.

$450.00 - 500.00

When a gentle, mild husband with a primitives-oriented mate examined a weathered rough pine carpenter's desk, his vehement reaction was, "If my wife brought that thing home, I'd leave."

Thus, there are those who crave as others cringe at the mention of country furniture, but the homey, distressed-from-use items reminiscent of the lives of generations of ordinary people in the past hold allure for many. They help transform kitchens, recreation rooms, bedrooms, dining areas, and living rooms into "personality places" which reflect back while serving the present, linking heritage with now, gluing together the generation gap. One addict commented, "If we can help acquaint our youth with their ancestors through antique acquisitions, our collections will be worthwhile." These time-was articles are chunks of history, a visual social studies venture.

There are other pro arguments. A "modern," addicted to elaborate Victorian walnut and cherry, toured a house where rustic pieces were dominant, and afterwards remarked, "People who like country furniture are warm, outgoing, casual, and relaxed." She acknowledged that such a decor would not suit her. Perhaps that is why interior designers maintain a home should accentuate you, framing your personality, with colors and textures chosen to complement you. If country furniture and primitives generate a glow, include them in the decorating scheme.

In addition to enjoyment, some collectors are aware of the economic value. As one woman stated, "Antiques are going up in price all the time. No way am I going to encourage my son to buy a reproduction which will cost as much or more, and what'll he have? It will depreciate and be secondhand while an antique will increase in worth."

Antiques are one of the world's leading businesses currently. Furnishings of the common person of the past cross economic boundary lines to be appreciated and collected by affluent as well as impecunious buyers.

Above: Carpenter's desk, pine, lift top, drop lid, original red paint. Size: 43" wide, 19" deep, 42" high.

$275.00 - 325.00

Right: Hutch, also called a settle or chair table; poplar, lift lid storage compartment, oak holding pins for top. Size: base: 29" wide, 18" deep; table top: 41½" wide, 25¾" deep.

$750.00 - 900.00

Country Furniture Defined

These are some pro and con statements which make discussion of the topic "What is country furniture?" apropos. Definitions differ. Early country furniture was primarily utilitarian, made from necessity to fit a particular need; generally crafted at home, by hand, out of native woods, found in rural regions or on the frontier; and most was unadorned, often quaint, in the simplicity of its design. Much was the work of the tinkering-at-all-trades farmer.

Some examples embrace mass-mades, such as Hitchcock-type chairs with fancy decorations (from the 1820s - 1840s on); or the cottage suites, manufactured in the 1870s at many factories, including those at Grand Rapids, Michigan, the last century's furniture capital of the United States. Stenciled flowers, fruits, or birds burst forth in an attempt to imitate nature's beauty on chests of drawers, commodes, or bed head and foot boards. Other furniture, simple in tone, such as plain kitchen cupboards and wardrobes, deserves mention.

Hitchcock-type chair, pillow top rail, cornucopia slat with stenciled gold fruits, rush seat. Size: 17" to seat, 33¼" high.
$225.00 - 275.00

Cottage-type lift top stenciled commode, pine and poplar, artificial graining, false drawer on left. Size: 28" wide, 16" deep, 32" high.
$275.00 - 325.00

Primitives Defined

Primitives are closely akin to country, the twain tending to overlap; yet, customarily primitives are the cruder, functional items from the past, the early ones hand fashioned when a need arose. If a family lived in an isolated area, someone had to make whatever was required in the best way he or she knew how, often with limited tools. Later, non-furniture articles such as washing machines, wringers, butter churns, or water pumps embrace factory-mades from the turn-of-the-century. These often were secured from mail order houses, but are now obsolete. They hold a nostalgic pull for those who remember the one grandpa and grandma had. These newer items may not meet the one-hundred-year-old qualifying standard of the United States government for antiques, but presently they attract consumer attention and are serving as conversation pieces in homes.

For the purpose of this book, rustic articles such as those from stores, barns, or peculiar to various occupations will be considered also. This broad definition of both country and of primitives—cottage, not castle-type furnishings — is loose and free, generously incorporating many articles which can be inspected at shops, flea markets, antique shows, or malls. Our definition includes items of collectible age which are of interest and passé, but not legally antique centenarians.

Woodworkers selected various fruitwoods (including cherry), or took oak, walnut, hickory, ash, beech, butternut, gum, sycamore, cedar, chestnut, but many stereotype specific light species, especially pine and maple, as country. Some include poplar, which can range from greenish gray or light to dark; but actually many kinds of this nation's indigenous woods were employed to construct items with a rustic feel, the majority of the output plainly designed.

Right: Washtub holder and wringer, maple, patented Nov. 19, 1901, White Diamond name. Size: 45" wide, 16" deep, 49" high.

$75.00 - 110.00

Below: Chopping block, pine, splayed legs, 2½" thick top. Size: 34" wide, 18¼"-22" deep, 26½" high.

$120.00 - 150.00

Bench, pine, splayed legs go through top of bench and are wedged to hold. Size: 54" wide, 11" deep, 16" high.

$70.00 - 90.00

Country Furniture Could Copy Classical Styles

Even though country furniture was primarily functional, built to meet needs rather than to appease aesthetic appetites, at times an attempt was made to simulate the current city styles or to follow period designs that the English cabinetmakers such as Chippendale, Hepplewhite, or Sheraton popularized in the late 1700s and early 1800s. Some furniture created as simplified copies of these masters' efforts maintains a quiet grace, depending on the skill of the maker. Other examples of period pieces a la country appear cumbersome and ungainly.

Such furnishings as bed frames, desks, cradles, washstands, cupboards, trunks, pie safes, tubs and buckets, dry sinks, plain sideboards — all can meet the functional home crafter criteria. Datewise survival colonial pieces from the 1600s are rare and rate a museum quality ranking while very few furnishings from the 1700s are available. Therefore, this book stresses products (mainly pine) of the 1800s, including factory made, with a rustic appeal.

Historically, in 1798, Eli Whitney, the inventor of the cotton gin, developed machinery to stamp out identical parts for muskets for the United States government, showing that guns no longer had to be hand crafted individually. His introduction of interchangeable parts started the idea of mass production. By 1808, Eli Terry's shop turned out hundreds of clocks with machinery Terry himself designed, and Lambert Hitchcock placed chairs on the market in the 1820s, which represented this country's first mass produced furniture. This indicates that factory furniture has been available for over one hundred and fifty years, so it's erroneous to think that a chest or desk from the 1800s is always a handmade article. Inexpensive cottage-type factory wares were available to last century's hoi polloi. Factory furniture could include hand touches, however.

But, there were also pioneer families who tended to be self-sustaining, self-supporting units alone, farmer craftsmen, jack-of-all trades, who employed simple tools such as axes for chopping; frows (or froes) to slice shingles; mauls (heavy

Desk, cedar and walnut, old glass pulls with brass backing, cabriole legs. Made from cedar tree on South Dakota family farm. Size: 42½" wide, 19½" deep, 31¼" high.
$350.00 - 400.00

hammers or mallets) to pound with; knives for cutting and carving; or an adze (adz), a wood scraping or shaving tool similar to an ax but with a crosswise blade, to transform the native trees into homes and household items. Other tools could include saws, chisels, and gouges to cut and shape wood plus planes to level or smooth it, squares to measure straight angles, a scribing gauge to mark with, calipers to measure thickness, hand worked lathes to make turnings, gimlets for boring, and drills; but few frontiersmen owned so much equipment. They made do with what they had available, but many handmade furnishings were well constructed because they have lasted until the current generation. Customarily unembellished with inlay and carving, the plain lines can be attractive, depending on the ability of their unknown originator as he manipulated his unsophisticated tools. When cabinetmakers arrived to settle in backwoods areas, they too usually kept their articles functional and unpretentious.

Some would close the classification of country furniture there. Others would stretch it to include farmyard features such as grain measures, milk stools, wagon or buggy seats, goat milking stalls, and egg crates. Various occupations are not neglected either. Apothecary leavings, confectionary tables and seats, tavern tables, printers' boxes, dental cabinets, barbershop left-overs, smithy furnishings of a bulky nature or over-sized bellows substituting as coffee tables, macabre articles from funeral parlors, carpenters' chests, cobbler benches, as well as those used by harness makers may limbo under the primitive line. The general store stuff such as spool or tobacco cabinets, desks for thread, coffee bins, advertising items, or display cases can sneak in. Since the definitions of country furniture can vary, this book will consider farm objects, store props, and occupational reminders adopted for home display, but will segregate them from actual articles constructed as furniture.

Wood box, pine, three different size wood compartments.
Size: 39" wide, 14" deep, 30" high.
$95.00 - 120.00

Blacksmith's table, maple, 2 copper bands nailed around edge. Size: 35" diameter, 23¼" high.
$200.00 - 250.00

Chapter 2
Antiques: Facts, Fakes, and Foibles

The next problem which confronts those afflicted with country-itis is — how to distinguish the true from the false. Antiquers speak of "marriages," "cobbled pieces," "reproductions," and "fakes." What do these words mean and how can the novice understand them, especially when the chronic answer seems to be summed up by the word "experience"? The hefty anvil salesman in "The Music Man" drama proclaims loudly, "Ya gotta know the territory." So — "You've gotta know the feel and look of antiques," the neophyte is told, but how? Association, being around the old, aids greatly. Visits to museums and antique shows or shops and research in books help, but since much rustic furniture was homemade to fit a particular need which may not exist today, there can be distinct, one-of-a-kind articles. This means a study of examples serves merely as a guide. To begin, consider the definition of each of the preceding terms.

Antique Marriages Defined

Many in the trade employ the word "marriage" to designate unrelated items which are joined together to become one unit. Antique marriages of two distinct pieces of furniture are not formed in heaven, but are at times inaugurated for profit by someone who attempts to supply a more appealing product to the

Above: Drysink, pine, wainscoted doors. Size: 49" wide, 20" deep, 40½" high. This is a cobbled piece. The backboard is newer looking pine which has been stained. You can see and feel where the little drawer was added.   **$225.00 - 250.00**

Left: Corner cupboard and base, pine. Top size: 32" wide, 16" deep, 48" high. Base size: 54" wide, 25" deep, 35¾" high. These two cupboards are marked and priced separately in a shop, but if somone united them, they would represent a marriage.

Top: $245.00 - 275.00   Bottom: $225 - 260.00

buying public. Vintage bookshelves are placed on a topless desk base to form a secretary; a sideboard (buffet) lacks an ornate back and one from something else is supplied; a set of legs is combined with an elderly top to make a table. These mismatched pieces, frequently very compatible, constitute "marriages." When such a union was completed many years ago, it can be respectable and accepted by most collectors much as some places recognize common law people marriages as legal after a certain period of years lapse; but convenient combinations of recent origin tend to produce frowns from experts who resist such joinings.

"Cobbled" Defined

The "saleability" aspect may lure people to cut closed cupboards into open pewter ones of an earlier date or into dry sinks or desks, and since the wood is old with outmoded construction, these "cobbled-up" creations are foolers. While essential restoration is legitimate, most people scowl over cobbled works. Great Britain's Frederick Roe, one time editor of the "Connoisseur," wrote in the idiom of England in his book *Home Furnishings with Antiques.* This author suggests that someone who protests when a woven chair seat is replaced could be told that if he were three hundred years old "his own seat" might not be in "first rate repair." Recently, an owner of a circa 1800 rush seated rocker was concerned that its antique value would plunge if the bottom were redone. Maybe all he seeks to do is to look at his relic, which is fine; however, common sense decrees that, if he elects to use it, the weak seat requires replacing and such a necessary repair would not be considered a cobbled project. Authority Roe could suggest the owner's own bottom might take a plunge if he sits in his unrepaired chair.

In this same vein, remember that replacing internal stops for drawers or worn runners (drawer slides) will make your chest of drawers or desk more functional without destroying its lines. Use discrimination and be sensible about accepting functional repairs.

If an article is authentic and rare, it may receive many careful transplants to make it resemble what it once was. A midwestern dealer literally unearthed a William and Mary country table (in the United States, circa 1700-1725) in a deteriorated, below ground Pennsylvania fruit cellar. There was a hole in the top and the tired, centuries-old legs had some damage. This worthy ancestor with its historic past deserved the expensive tender loving attention it received since much of it had been preserved and museums coveted it. But generally, avoid pieces of a later date which require extensive repairs or replacements which are costly and leave you with a genuine, authentic nothing much.

Dresser, pine. Size: 40" wide, 18" deep, 44" high. This dresser had a veneer surface which was deteriorated and was removed to expose the pine underneath. The ogee curve of the top drawer is a clue that this was not originally a simple pine chest.
$275.00 - 300.00

Here's one unorthodox way to alter the appearance of a large veneered chest of drawers. Because of the difficulty in securing matching veneer for the restoration process, the owner may decide to strip off the veneer and reveal the base wood which is often pine or poplar. This can be accomplished by removing any finish such as varnish, paint, or stain. Next, a water-dampened cloth is placed over the veneer and a hot iron is set on it so that the resulting steam loosens the adhering glue beneath. The veneer in this treated area can be pried up gently with a blunt instrument such as a putty knife and the surface dried off with a cloth before proceeding to the next section, until the "denuding" reaches completion. Such tampering tattles on itself because customarily an original rural piece would have simple straight lines, while a veneered work tends to be a more elegant sophisticate with curves, swoops, and carvings. This is a cobbled job, and at times articles are offered for sale as pine when their veneer coats have been steamed away. The purchaser should be told about the transmutation. Of course, if someone were really a fraud, he could gentle the lines to make them emulate a plain style.

Ogee mirrors have a double continuous curve (S-like) and date back to the Empire Period (pre 1830). They were veneered richly. A favored way to secure a "country pine" frame is to strip the mahogany topping off to expose the underlayer. Ogee clocks, too, may be done in this manner so that their urban dark appearance changes to a paler rustic look. This is a common practice, and that double curve should immediately make you exclaim, "Ogee — this has been tampered with." Some people soak frames in a tub of water for an hour or so until the glue softens to release the veneer; then, they dry the surface with an absorbent cloth. That's faster than the steaming method. Frames with a plaster covering are treated in a similar fashion to uncover pine.

Reproductions Versus Fakes

While all down through the years copies have been made of articles which have successfully served past generations, current re-creations of antiques are known as "reproductions." Replicas made and sold as such would not be spurious unless they were offered as genuine centenarians in an attempt to defraud buyers. In contrast, the word "fake" implies knowingly misrepresenting an antique in any aspect. Attributing it falsely to a certain craftsman; identifying its age and style incorrectly; distorting its history; or concealing restorations or changes would fit under this classification.

Wash type bench, pine. Size: 28″ wide, 11½″ deep, 18″ high. The owner knows that this little bench is a twenty year old reproduction. It is joined by brads and has no patina.
$50.00 - 65.00

Rush seat rocker, maple. Size: 14½" to seat; 35¾" to top. The rush seat in the rocker was replaced to make it useable. Common sense decrees some restoration work may be required on antiques.
$120.00 - 150.00

Oval mirror, pine. Size: 14½" x 12". The plaster of paris which originally covered this frame was soaked off so the pine underneath would be exposed for a rustic feel. Note the dovetailed construction.
$60.00 - 75.00

Hanging shelf, pine. Size: 24" wide, 7" deep, 32" high. Although an ideal shelf for some lovely pewter pieces, this shelf was recently constructed from packing box wood.
$45.00 - 65.00

Detecting Alterations

So how does one detect detracting alterations? Thoroughly inspect a piece before you buy it, using a flashlight, if necessary. Check inside, outside, back, front, sides, upside down, drawers, hardware, underneath the top. Often a replaced section can be noted because wood of a different thickness, coloration, or grain pattern can be seen. Parts not original with edges cut to fit, appearing paler and showing current workmanship, would indicate change. Cabinetmakers did mix woods, so the use of various woods is not a conclusive indication by itself. Some bend better, yield additional strength, carve easier, possess greater beauty, are less expensive for side pieces where the wood doesn't show much, or some makers used up what they had available and stained or painted all to match. Because of this, the species of wood utilized is a rough guide; however, major components should be of the same thickness and age. The rough edges should have a similar feel and appearance, be darkened, and not look newly cut.

Sometimes decorations of two "married" pieces differ — the top may have carved turnings and applied designs (glued or nailed-on ornaments) while the base could have incised lines on it, which tends to indicate that the twain are not compatible. Reason would decree that a top with scalloped edges would not fit with a base featuring scrolls, but there must have been country cabinetmakers who mixed and mis-matched styles, almost as fashions now combine plaids, stripes, and florals in one garment or in home decors, a practice which once would have been termed gauche.

Hardware tells tales of switches. It is possible to discern where screws, or such things as hinges in a drop leaf table, were fit into a different place and the original marks remain. There may be additional holes where other handles once were, or a little ridge outline of these pulls can be seen on the wood from a dirt or wax build-up. The area underneath a removed handle would have a lighter outline because the surface has been protected from the exposure which darkens wood. Seek and ye shall find.

Detecting Age in Furniture

"I don't know how to tell when something is really old. I wanted to buy an antique set for my dining room but was afraid I'd get taken so I bought modern instead," a young woman declared recently.

An attempt was made to show her how to spot outmoded construction, but if she lacks courage, she should not invest in vintage articles. Most people make some unwise purchases (or pass up a treasure) especially when they are beginners, but learning is a constant, continuing process. Here are a few aids to assist collectors-to-be.

Schoolmaster's desk, pine, poplar, soft maple. Size: 44" wide, 16" deep, 29" high. This desk is a marriage. The top is old. The legs came from a table, and the corner apron supports are made from newer wood, stained dark.

$175.00 - 225.00

Dry sink cupboard, pine. Size: 40" wide, 14½" deep, 49½" high. Replaced hinges and a replaced door catch are signs of alterations. Notice the outline of the original door catch.

$350.00 - 375.00

Patina Defined

It is important to recognize the natural wearing and aging process of wood which causes the color to deepen. That's called patina, and it should be evenly distributed over surfaces equally exposed to the air, light, and dust. The underside of a piece can be revealing because such places as the bottom of the last drawer in a chest or desk gets more exposure than its counterpart, the bottom of the top drawer; thus, the former should be darker than the latter. The insides of such case pieces should not have a new appearance but should have mellowed with use. Patina develops slowly over a period of time with a same all over appearance on outer surfaces, while if stain is utilized to emulate this look, it may not be even in color. People may try orange shellac but it stands on the surface and might have an occasional drip. It would be all over the same, even where less air and light touches the piece on inner portions and paler deepening would be anticipated. Painting a raw surface with an ammonia-plug tobacco blend, which has stood combined for several days to mix well, is harder to detect since it seeps in, but normally, a consistent deeper color with a mellow aspect suggests "old."

Signs of Wear

Time causes edges to tend to wear smooth and sharp features to soften; therefore, watch for genuine signs of wear. Friction causes the bottom edges of drawers to wear away unevenly — more in the middle — from the constant abrasive moving across the runners caused by multi-openings and closings through the years. Chair rungs become scooped out on top when feet continually rest on them. Chairs are frequently dragged about so that their leg bottoms are rarely perfectly flat. "Don't lean back in that chair!" is a housewifely command often unheeded. As a result a finial may be worn from wall contact where a man has tilted back repeatedly, and a chair leg can be correspondingly smoothed off at the rear from such lounging. A broom hits the base of a low-slung piece and leaves slight mars, especially on soft woods; a dust rag in time softens outer edges;

Plank chair, undetermined woods. Notice the signs of wear on this chair – the front turned rung has been worn flat and the paint is worn off in spots.

$65.00 - 85.00

Pennsylvania rocker, undetermined woods. Size: 20″ x 20″ seat, 41″ to top. The paint on the arms has been worn off by constant rubbing, and the seat and back have faded from body contact.

$300.00 - 325.00

18

and consistent scrubbing of kitchen or dining table tops shows with almost a bleaching aspect. The places where hands consistently touch an article will be worn, such as the arms of a chair where spots of bare wood may appear, smoothed by constant caressing; or around the pulls on drawers and doors. On a painted or artificially grained item, there have to be some imperfections and muting of colors caused by use and handling. The flowers or fruits stencil design on a chair slat or splat is going to be worn in an uneven manner by constant contact with the sitter's back against it, and the seat hues grow dimmer from bodily contact. Painted trunks experience the laying on of many hands as their lids are forced open and banged shut and consequently indicate special wear at those spots. Look for wear where it should appear and suspect any in doubtful locations.

Pegs Have a Purpose

Some women joyfully squeal, "Oh, it's pegged!" when they notice dowels used in the construction of furniture. Pegs must have a purpose. Do the dowels meet a need: for example, to hold a drawer together or to join panels on a door or to reinforce a joint? Pegs are not round but are more squarish when hand fashioned and are not exactly precise in size. In the late 1800s and early 1900s machinery-constructed drawers frequently featured perfect circle pegs, and these should not be confused with the non-round oldies. Occasionally, pegs are pounded into odd places for show in attempt to imitate passe work and they have no reason to be there. Remember, pegs must be functional, needed to hold two pieces together, in order to be considered legitimate.

Four drawer bureau commode, butternut. Size: 26" wide, 13" deep, 32" high. Although the handles or pulls on furniture may be metal, ceramic, glass, or wood, they are still termed hardware. These porcelain knobs are an example of hardware.

$225.00 - 250.00

Open cupboard, pine. Size: 36½" wide, 16" deep, 71" high. Notice hand planed panel on door and pegs adding strength to the mortise and tenoned construction. Marked in black script "Made 1863 by F. Sager."

$650.00 - 725.00

Hardware Helps

Hardware is helpful. Oddly, the pulls or handles on furniture may be made of metal, ceramic, glass, wood; yet, this term can encompass them all as well as escutcheons (outlines around keyholes or back plates for bale handles), and hinges. Early manufacturers supplied articles with or without handles since hardware was expensive and many purchasers preferred to furnish their own. The list price fluctuated accordingly. Mirrors (referred to as toilets in late 1800 catalogs) were optional. (Washing, dressing, and combing hair are part of one's toilet; hence, the archaic term for a looking glass.) This means that chests or dressers might never have had mirrors attached and also allows for a great variety of handles, sometimes handmade when the furniture is not. Hardware includes nails or screws also.

When a young couple began their quest for antiques, they refinished a battered chest without handles, and put reproduced metal pulls on it. An antique dealer saw their work and remarked, "That's a good commode washstand, but that's not the correct hardware." The wife was indignant. "How can she tell? She wasn't close enough to inspect it." After becoming more accustomed to antiques, these newcomers could sight such discrepancies themselves. They had put Queen Anne handles with ornate "brass" back plates and bales (circa 1725-1750) on an 1870s piece which should have had "tear drop" pulls or carved wooden ones. The two were as incongruous as high heels with roller skates. Wooden peg pulls, whittled pulls, and round flattened wooden knobs, or on occasion, white porcelain types frequently accompany simple furniture, while door catches are often wooden tongues which twist to fit into a prong. Both immediately before and after 1900, country oriented styles could feature machined cast metal rectangles open at the bottom to offer a hand grip and angular catches — all bearing a similar stamped design. It is not amiss to find carved fruit or acorn pulls or tear drops on rustic pieces; and leather or iron handles are good companions for trunks and chests.

The blacksmith, a respected skilled workman, heated, shaped, and hammered out iron hinges, handles, and hasp fastenings for doors or lids whose variations indicate they are "hand dones," not precisely alike.

Keyhole outlines (escutcheons) may be of iron, brass, wood, bone, or ivory, and certain types are associated with various periods but are not positive indications of age as they can be duplicated or owners may change the hardware. However, escutcheons are less apt to be switched than handles, which are constantly pulled and tugged to receive more wear or are subject to replacement when someone seeks to modernize a vintage piece.

Occasionally a lock bears a patent date which tells you it was constructed sometime in or after the year indicated, not the precise date it was made, as patents exist for a period of time.

Next, consider screws. Early ones, fashioned of brass or iron, were probably first used around 1690 and had blunt ends, no points, flat, not perfect circle heads, and grooves or spirals which were not precisely even. 1700s Brass, an alloy composed of copper, zinc, and perhaps some tin, might have less copper and retain more of a yellowish-white cast than a golden glow. There were machine-made screws available around 1800 (give or take a decade) which were more regular, had sharper edges, but kept the flat tips. Modern manufactured screws with their sharp points, symmetrical threads, and precisely divided round heads with deeper screwdriver slots date to the mid-1800s.

Nails too have gone through an evolutionary period with early ones square-headed or with irregular bumps appearing in the 1600s and 1700s. Handwrought examples were tapered to a bluntish point on all four sides and of good quality iron that endured. Usually they were not inset into the wood and were not perfectly spaced when pounded into the surface. If they have not been replaced, the wood tends to darken in a halo around them and sort of swell over them a trifle. In 1786, Ezekiel Reed of Massachusetts created a machine to cut nails which were flat, tapering on two sides to a point. By the late 1860s, a steel version with a round head was available, and in the 1890s, today's wire nail with a round head, pointed tip, and a round body emerged. Remember, it is possible to purchase square heads today, so again, one clue is not conclusive. As in a jigsaw puzzle, it is only when all the parts are put together that an age picture appears.

Trunk, pine. Size: 30" wide, 16" deep, 16" high. Metal strapping held by brass headed nails adds design and strength to this "loaf of bread" trunk. Large brass or iron escutcheons appear on trunks dating in the 1800 s. **$145.00 - 175.00**

Utility carrying box, pine, dovetailed corners. Size: 16" wide, 9" deep, 11" high. The red paint has been retained on this 1800 utility box.

$65.00 - 85.00

Lift top commode, pine, originally artificially grained. Size: 29" wide, 17" deep, 32½" high. Round knobs and wooden door fasteners were common hardware on country chests of the mid 1800 s.

$275.00 - 325.00

21

Preserve that Paint

And then there's paint. It is said that latter day pioneers created their own by blending together leftovers such as coffee grounds or excess eggs. When the family owned a cow and it gave more milk than was consumed, the extra was thrown in as an attempt was made to find a lasting base. Clay, berry juice, or blood from butchering edible animals provided a red pigment to concoct a durable inexpensive coating which could be applied generously to furniture. Some sources state that red, green, black, and yellow were 1600 hues while the now-faded, famed milk paint reds, blues, or grays emerged as the 1700s terminated.

Indigo from India was costly to import, but there were those who sought this blue tone. In the 1740s and 50s and for about one hundred years thereafter, South Carolina and Georgia grew indigo plants, a member of the pea family. In 1897, a synthetic was developed from aniline, a coal-tar product, and the natural plant dye became outmoded. Today specialized collectors treasure the faded red and paling blue of long ago as representative of a specified time in American history, preserving it diligently, a practice which has merits both antique and heritage wise. Others don't appreciate this chipped, cracked worn sign of age and scrape

Trunk, pine, dovetailed corners, original blue paint and dated 1889. Size: 36" wide, 18" deep, 21" high.

$175.00 - 200.00

China cabinet, butternut, stained and decorated with a sponge. Notice the drawer on the right was stripped and restained as if someone meant to refinish the piece. Originally a pie cupboard with punched tin panels that have been replaced with glass. Size: 43½" wide, 17½" deep, 52" high.

$375.00 - 425.00

Bench, pine, splayed legs extend through top. Old pine takes on a battered look and it is not unusual to find burn marks where a candle or lantern fell over; gouges, splits, and indentations are common. Size: 28" wide, 10"-10-¾" deep, 13½" high.

$75.00 - 95.00

or paint-remove down to the bare wood, determined to refinish their furnishings naturally, despite the fact that they were not available originally with their light pine or grayish green poplar showing. Those with removers or scrapers in hand should be aware that a small amount of the old finish should be saved in inconspicuous places to help determine dates and to help insure that all parts are original. There are those who retain but touch up the old finish for a fresher appearance, thus tinkering with time and to some, tarnishing value, while others accept this practice as legitimate. However, for the seekers, here is a recipe for milk paint which dates back to at least 1879.

Milk Paint — for barns, any color. Mix water lime with skim-milk to proper consistency to apply with brush, and it is ready for use. It will adhere well to wood, smooth or rough, to brick, mortar, or stone, where oil has not been used, and forms a very hard substance as durable as the best oil paint. Any color may be had by using colors dissolved in whisky (sic).

From Ransom's Family Receipt Book
1879, Free to Everyone
Published by D. Ransom, Son & Co.
Buffalo, N.Y.

An up-to-date formula calls for powdered milk mixed with water until a paint-like consistency results, with the desired dry color secured at a paint or art supply store added. Bright tones can be dulled for an old look by including brown or black pigment, the amount necessary determined by experimentation. These paints are akin to glues which include a casein base. Casein is a protein which is present in milk.

Don't assume something is elderly simply because it is painted and battered. Aged paint tends to flake off in brittle chips while layers of new are more pliable as they peel, and they may smell fresh. It is possible to distress a wooden surface with hammers, rasps, or chains to give it a beat-up appearance. Worm holes, actually the larvae of beetles, are not an age indicator either since "bugs" can enter wood at any time, and if a thin dust is present, beware. There may be something chomping away on the wood at the present time. The holes come in different pin-prick sizes and infestation occurs in one location more than others so the distribution on the surface would not be equal or precisely spaced. If holes are cut through, they will zigzag and such an appearance might suggest the replacement of a part. A wire inserted into a hole won't plunge in if meandering, typical of a "worm" is present, thus manifesting falsified holes.

The Joiner's Joints

Here's another thought. Do you realize that glue is new — well, relatively so? It was not commonly utilized until the late 1700s. And, are you aware that a "joiner" was not a term originally for a socializer who delights in belonging to many organizations? Rather, he was a craftsman of yore who would parallel the latter day cabinetmaker. In this man's vocabulary, a "joint" was the way two pieces of wood were attached to hold solidly in the construction of furniture. This he accomplished without the aid of glue or metal. No nails, no screws were employed. When an apprentice became a master at this work, he was awarded the title "joiner." Later, the name "cabinetmaker" was applied to the men who, to the horror of the joiners, took glue, screws, nails, and metal fastenings to help hold their furniture creations together. Carpenters also included furniture making in their trade way back in the times of the joiners, and this tradition has continued through the years. Perhaps you've wondered why undertakers sometimes sell furniture, a combination which dates back to a prior time when men who made home furnishings also sawed out coffins and the two jobs became entwined in frontier locales or small towns. Screws, nails, or glue were not always available in remote areas so time-tested joining methods were utilized for many years by the farmer-craftsman.

Now, if one follows orthodox joiner methods, what types of joints does he prefer? Some examples follow.

Mortise and tenon   The mortise is a slot or hole. The tenon is a tongue or thick prong, usually with shoulders on at least two sides, cut to extend out on a piece of wood so that it can be fit snugly into a corresponding size slot or hole (mortise) in another wooden piece. The mortise may be made of unseasoned lumber and the tenon of seasoned so that as the hole section dries out, it will shrink and grip the tongued portion (already shrunken) more tightly. A wooden pin is driven through the union to assure that they will adhere to each other permanently. Such a joint is easy to detect because it is found in all periods of American furniture. Examine a bed. In many cases, the posts will have slots into which projecting prongs on the head and foot boards will fit. The slats on chair backs are inserted into the posts in that same manner. The aprons on tables or chests of drawers may be joined in like fashion.

Single drop leaf table, pine; an example of a rustic joiner's work with a mortise and open tenon on legs, square pegs in use, and dovetails showing on the drawer edge. Size: 28¼" wide, 41" deep with leaf in extended position, 24" high.

$275.00 - 300.00

Wedge

In some instances, a wedge, a piece of wood which tapers to a thin edge, might be driven into the tenon after it is in place to force it apart, the resulting expansion permitting a very snug fit in the slot or hole.

Inspect a chair in which the legs extend up through and show on the top of the seat. A wedge frequently was pounded in to cause the end of the leg to expand and form a tight joint. Early Windsor chairs from the 1700s were made sturdy in this manner. The arm supports may be set in sockets drilled all the way through a seat and the use of a wedge would help secure them in place. When the end of a tenon can be seen, it may be referred to as open, and that is when a wedge can be inserted.

Tongue and groove

When a continuous tongue sticks out at the end of a board and is inserted into a corresponding groove cut into the wooden piece to which it is to be united, it is called a tongue and groove joint.

The wainscoting displayed on many dry sinks would be an example of tongue and groove construction.

Lap or rabbet joint

Alternate boards may be cut so that a right angle in the front of one slips into a right angle cut in the back of another to make a smooth fit. This is referred to as a rabbet or lap joint. At times a right angle cut at the end of one board is positioned to overlap the edge of another straight board.

Drawers from the late 1600s might have a rabbet joint. A peg or hand wrought nail could be driven in for additional holding power.

The backs of case pieces are frequently made of a series of boards which are united edge to edge by right angle notches.

Butt joint

In a butt joint, two straight edges of wood are pushed against each other (butted together). Early joiners would peg them to keep them in position. Later workers tended to use glue or nails. Nails can work out and do not hold well, yet many people think of them as the repair-it-all and pound them in any place, often splitting the wood carelessly.

Six board chests are lift lid boxes consisting of two ends, two sides, a top, and a bottom — six boards. They commonly had simple butt joints.

Not all old drawers were dovetailed. Butt joints were utilized also.

Miter joint

When the ends of two boards which are to be joined are cut at a slant so that they can be matched together to form a right angle, the result is called a miter joint. A peg was driven through both pieces to secure them.

Rectangular and square picture frames, mirrors, and moldings may show this type of construction at the corners.

Dovetail joint

Dovetails, supposedly resembling the spread tail of a dove, are triangular shapes cut in one piece of wood to match a corresponding opening in another piece. They interlock in much the same manner as parts of jigsaw puzzles do. Before the machines of the 1800s took over, a joiner fashioned his by hand. He took a sharp pointed instrument and "scribed" or incised guide lines in the wood to indicate the size and spacing he desired to achieve.

He also scratched a straight line to show where the dovetails should end, and for the unskilled, it was easier to make a few large ones than a series of dainty ones. Such marks which helped match two pieces indicate hand workmanship since machines do not require similar assistance to make their precise, even dovetails.

The front and sides of drawers are often joined with the aid of dovetails, and boxes and trunks frequently feature this type of interlocking. The sides and top of case pieces can be dovetailed. Remember, while many drawers do have this type of construction, other joints were utilized also, including the lap or rabbet, and a butt style.

Tools of Yore Help Designate Age

Tools of yore left distinctive marks which help declare that a piece was not spawned currently by a machine. For example, the cuttings made by a saw are referred to as kerf marks, and before the mid-1800s, these would be in up and down parallel rows, indicating that a straight blade was employed to bite its teeth into the wood. Anticipate curved, almost semicircular, rows of lines when a circular saw did the work. This tool probably immigrated to the United States in about the 1820s and got around most places by the 1850s. If the two types of kerf marks are intermixed on one piece, suspect that a bit of hanky-panky might have occurred to unite two unassociated pieces as one.

Lathes which held a piece of wood and turned it against a cutting tool which shaped it were hand operated and did not rotate rapidly; thus, it is possible to see or feel narrow gougings on the resulting legs, finials, or posts. Since cabinetmakers were apt to judge the accuracy of their designs by comparing them with their eyes, each turned piece varies to some degree, an indication of a made-by-hand stamp of approval.

Calipers measure diameters and thicknesses, and when the turnings of a handmade chair are examined with these instruments, no two will be exactly alike sizewise. Instead, each leg on a chair will vary slightly in thickness and design.

Early jack planes made waves across the grain of the wood they sought to smooth or remove some portions of, and this can be felt on surfaces worked by hand. Sometimes it is possible to see these with-the-grain ripples.

Molding (a continuous ornamental edging applied to or carved in wood) made by hand with a plane was inclined to be plain on country furnishings. The applied type (added on) could be fastened with pegs or brads. When molding was machine made, the surface is regular; while unevenness, detected by sighting with one eye squinched shut lined up along the edge, is apparent on hand mades.

Differences might be considered clue number one when one seeks to learn whether a farmer-craftsman or a machine fashioned an article. Hand carving will waver a bit, and there will be slight variations.

Markings also are important. A home craftsman wants to be sure he will know where and how to cut or assemble a piece of wood before he actually does the work; therefore, he uses a sharp instrument to mark or scratch lines to direct him. These incised lines in the wood are evidence that a factory did not produce the furniture because machines don't require guidelines. Expect to find such indications at spots where two pieces join, such as where the slats of a chair fit into the posts or where the rungs are inserted into the legs. Hand done dovetail joints on a drawer will be outlined by a scriber. These are readily detectable signs of hand workmanship.

Church cabinet, pine; probably an ecclesiastical piece, as the top is finished and it was meant to sit on the floor. The cornice molding is slightly out of line, indicating hand workmanship. Size: 52¼" wide, 17" deep, 28¾" high.

$450.00 - 500.00

Bedside table, pine. The legs of this table all vary slightly in shape. Someone held a piece of wood to a hand operated lathe and guessed at the size and shape of the turnings. Size: 22½" wide, 21" deep, 27" high.

$175.00 - 200.00

Chair, maple and hickory, bamboo-like turnings, Shaker type; a craftsman would use a scribe to mark where he wished to incise the lines to represent bamboo turnings on the legs.

$125.00 - 150.00

Thick Wood of Random Widths Says Old

Thickness of boards and their width frequently spell "a—g—e." It doesn't have to be true, but much of the wood found in antiques is an inch or so thick, and if veneer (a thin layer of ornamental wood glued on top of a cheaper species) covers the surface, it could be so much as 1/8th an inch thick, while that employed today can be 1/32nd or considerably less — sometimes thin enough that 50 slices are made from an inch of wood. When genuine wood (not pressed forms or plastic imitations) is utilized on pieces today, the boards are generally 7/8th or 16/25th of an inch, the standard thickness. Boards can be obtained in widths of even numbers ranging from 6 to 12 inches. When boards of standard width and thickness appear in construction, think new, especially when a series of boards of exact measurement form a top. This was not true years ago when a top or a side might be made all of one piece or of one large and one small board. Random sizes were normal. Early legs, too, could be turned out of one piece while later ones might have layers of wood glued together before being turned. There was plenty of wood available, and it was cut generously and cheaply. When trees were scarcer and conservation became a political theme, wood was more expensive and stress was laid on using less lumber to help preserve the dwindling forests.

Does Shrinkage Tell Age?

Most authorities state that wood shrinks across the grain with age so that gaps will occur on table tops or backs of case pieces which have been made of a series of boards butted together. They also measure round tops to see if they are slightly elliptical, with a smaller distance across the grain than going with it; however, an internationally known expert with the United States Department of Agriculture Forest Products Laboratory who was consulted casts doubts on this latter premise, saying that a wooden bowl will often shrivel until it has an expanding crack when the weather is dry. When there is moisture in the air, the two pieces will swell and meet again. This can happen to a split side on a chest of drawers, and factors such as these lend credence to this forestry employee's words that he doubts shrinkage across the grain is a reliable indicator of age. His feelings about this are akin to those of others who discredit patina as a valid clue.

Glass can offer an assist to age hunters. Early cupboards tended to be the open type, having no doors. If panes of glass appeared, there would be a series of small ones separated and held by vertical wooden dividers called muntins because

Wood box, pine; a wood box was a utilitarian piece frequently constructed of different sized pieces of wood. A butt construction was used on this one. Size: 26½" wide, 17" deep, 36" high.

$150.00 - 200.00

it was not until the last half of the Victorian period that a method for making sheet glass in large pieces was developed. Glass from the colonial period was hand blown (by human lung power) and the hot glob of metal (as the molten glass was termed) left a bump in the center of the pane that many call a "bull's eye." Impurities in the silica (sand) used in the formula tended to produce a greenish cast to the resulting glass. Finding any such panes would be a rarity, and it would be extremely unusual if all of those required to make a door remained intact, without being broken and replaced, down through the years. During much of the 1800s glass panes were characterized by a wavy appearance, and collectors treasure this distorted look. Again, some replacement would be anticipated after years of use.

Cupboard, pine, two piece, six panes of glass are separated by muntins. Size: 40" wide, 18" deep, 75" high.

$650.00 - 700.00

Furniture Styles Help Determine Age

A knowledge of furniture styles and types helps indicate when a piece is aged. If a film producer wants to depict a teen-age girl of the 1940-World War II period, the actress frequently is dressed in white ankle socks and saddle shoes, a skirt that reaches to the middle of her knees, a white tailored blouse and a button -front, long-sleeved sweater. Her deeply permanent-curled hair bounces about at just above the shoulder. Immediately people picture the forties. Likewise certain types of furniture and woods experience periods of popularity, especially in formal furnishings. For example, Empire (circa 1815-1840) favored mahogany. The Victorian Era (circa 1830-1900) has been designated the age of walnut with an overlapping of oak supremacy in the late 1800s which extended into the early decades of the 1900s. Patterns are not so easily traced in country types where a maker was apt to choose woods he had readily available and where simplicity was a keynote. Of course, successful styles are copied so this presents only a general standard. Pictures tell the tale better than words, so please examine the illustrations.

Smell the Age

If you have a beagle nose, use it to help you as you examine antiques. There is an old smell to something with a past, and if the purpose of the object is known, there may be a lingering odor. For example, a clinging cinnamon, clove, or gingery scent might accompany a spice box while a coffee grinder may have a bean fragrance. Fresh paint can smell new while that that has been around a while can be musty. Employ your beak to seek out antiques.

Back in grammar school days, a special speaker presented an auditorium program on street safety. He taught the primary grades a poem which they acted out in unison, terminating with a noisy stomping of feet. It went like this:

Stop, look and listen
Before you cross the street,
Use your eyes,
Use your ears,
And then use your feet.

An antiquer might paraphrase it this way:

Stop, use your senses
Before you buy antiques,
Use your eyes
Use your hands,
And then use your beak.

Left: Scandinavian coffee grinder, pine, wrought iron handle, door swings up for inserting beans. A coffee odor may cling to an antique grinder. Old wood smells old, sometimes with a mustiness adhering to it.
$85.00 - 95.00

So, to summarize, give consideration to all the guides as you inspect possible old-fashioned acquisitions. See, feel, and smell the difference. The clues to honest age are there if you seek to employ your senses before you spend a cent. Emulate the deductive reasoning of your favorite detective — Columbo, Sherlock Holmes, Ellery Queen, or one of Agatha Christie's greats. Additional assistance is provided by a sleuth's magnifying glass plus a flashlight when you seek to distinguish the genuine from the false or the pure from the cobbled.

Chapter 3
The Plumbing Problem

A young couple in the "just turned twenty" age bracket examined articles at an antique show and inquired about the price of a dry sink. The dealer assumed they meant a large one in the adjoining booth, and they were aghast at the cost of the kitchen piece with its tray for holding water, the forerunner of a modern sink. They were in error. They were actually asking about a common washstand, a table-type furnishing upon which a bowl and pitcher stood with a drawer for "toilet" sundries, open legs, and a shelf beneath for a slop jar. ("Toilet" in this case means the bathing and dressing process, including hair care.) Because of this misunderstanding, for the "we've always had plumbing" crowd, a few explanations are included about articles developed to meet specific water related needs back when aqua was carried into the home by people, not piped in.

To pioneers, water presented problems. Currently it is convenient to dash into the bathroom, turn, tug, twist, pull, or push on a faucet, and to have water, your choice — hot, cold, tepid — flow out; but time was when the availability of this vital liquid helped determine where frontier families settled. Streams offered transportation facilities; but more important, water was essential for drinking, cooking, cleansing, growing crops, and watering livestock. The chattering brooks, twisting creeks, and rushing rivers with their clear, ordinarily unpolluted contents furnished it, or springs oozing up from the ground became the supply source. When a homesteader had time, he could dig a well and with a long rope to which was attached a wooden bucket, that he could fashion readily from a hollow log, he could draw water manually up out of the earth. Later, hand operated pumps were inaugurated to pull up the water. At times it was necessary to prime a pump by pouring water into the top to start its action. This might be

Towel bar common washstand, pine. Size: 18" wide, 13½" deep, 32" high.

$175.00 - 200.00

Dry sink, pine. Size: 36" wide, 19" deep, 28" high.
$260.00 - 300.00

required in arid weather, or conversely, during a winter freeze. Youths liked to chide or dare a bumpkin to roll out his moist tongue to lick a pump in zero weather. How they would taunt when it froze to the iron surface since it was extremely painful to yield a slight bit of skin in order to pull the stuck tongue loose. In towns, pumps stood on street corners and anyone could fill a pail there, especially people without wells in their own yards or some whose might "run dry." Today, pumps with renewed vigor may have mail boxes attached, become address indicators, pose amid blooming posies, function as lamps, or form a rube's stage setting along with other yesterday items. "Gee, my grandmother had one. I wonder whatever happened to it?" is a nostalgic reminder that those days are history. Rain water caught off the roof in a cistern tank or in barrels didn't contain sulphur with its egg smell and taste or other minerals to make "hard water" as dug wells often did; thus, "soft water" was nature's own and not chemically induced — excellent for sudsy clotheswashing.

These days, it is simpler (and more pleasant) not to have to trek out to the "privy" in freezing weather when snow is knee-deep. However, there were times when it was convenient for a girl to escape dishwashing by suddenly needing a prolonged "backhouse" visit timed to terminate as the dish doing duty did, or a lazy lad lurked there to avoid chores. In the late 1800s or early 1900s the past issue of the mail order catalog (pre-dating squeeze-soft tissue) was kept in the outhouse for tear-off-a-sheet paper purposes. It could help a loafer, who didn't mind aromatic surroundings or seasonal cold and heat, pass the time away as he or she gazed at and coveted the enticingly described articles pictured in this "wish book." (One problem the advertisers didn't mention was how to obtain the hard-to-acquire finances to pay for these fabulous purchases.) Currently, since indoor plumbing has made outdoor toilets passe', today's fads often transform these little "necessaries" into swimming pool cabanas or, cut down, the top portions become child-size playhouses.

Washstand, pine. Size: 34¼" wide, 17½" deep, 35¼" high.

$220.00 - 250.00

Child's necessary chair on rockers, pine, hand grip for portability.
$125.00 - 150.00

In generations gone, the elite could have elaborate indoor bathrooms such as the one at Wheatland, President James Buchanan's estate in Lancaster, Pennsylvania. Upon his return following his residency in Washington, D. C. (1857-1861), Mr. Buchanan transformed his sitting area adjoining the master bedroom into a washroom modeled after the one at the White House with an over three feet deep zinc-lined wooden tub. Servants lugged hot water up the stairs to fill it while cold ran in from a tank on the third floor, possibly filled by rain caught as it ran off the roof. A large stand held two handsome porcelain bowls and pitchers, the smaller for cold, the larger for hot water. An oval container beneath cleansed feet. The wealthy could indulge in such extravagances. The hired help (or slaves in some locales prior to 1868) could dump and cleanse slop pots, but most people were not members of the prosperous, pampered populous, so for the poor, it was pot or path — the pot for shut-ins or for family nocturnal use, the path to the privy for able-bodied people.

In those days, the kitchen area, with its fireplace or cookstove, tended to be the warmest spot in the common-place home, and the wooden tub in which one sat in a knee-chest position was dragged out for Saturday night baths to be refilled for each family member in turn. On wash day, it could duplicate for clothes cleansing.

As late as the 1930s, or after that in remote rural locales, a kitchen wall shelf supported a wash basin; and hot water from the kettle, which always seemed to sit in a ready posture on the wood burning cookstove (range), could be poured into it. (Some ranges included reservoirs into which buckets of water were dumped to heat to keep a hot supply available when the stove fuel was glowing. This could be scooped out as needed for cleansing people, dishes, or floors.) Cold water dipped from an open pail would cool it to the proper temperature for shaving or hand washing. The same dipper served as a drinking vessel which everyone dunked into the bucket to fill and sip from — a communal container. In addition, there was a tin cup hanging at the water pump outside where anyone could imbibe at will — that one utensil available to all the thirsty — germs ignored through lack of knowledge of their existence. Accessory items to accompany the shelf were hanging wooden or tin cases, ranging from plain to elaborate, which kept combs available and might incorporate a mirror and/or a towel rack. Commonly, a harsh linen type towel revolved as one continuous unit on a wooden roller frame attached to the wall. When a spot became dirty or wet where hands and faces sloshed with water were wiped, the user yanked to cause a clean dry area to appear.

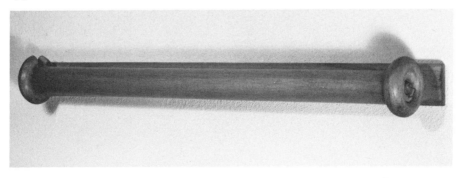

Towel rack roller, maple. Size: 21½" wide. $60.00 - 75.00

The same wash water, especially in periods of drought when conservation was imperative, served until it became murky and the contents would be poured into a "slop bucket" which waited nearby on the floor. When the receptacle became full, it would be dumped out-of-doors at some spot where there was little traffic so it would not cause mud problems. Frequently during dry spells, languishing plants profited from a dose of this waste liquid. At some periods in history bathing was shunned and labeled "unhealthy," and today's nightly ritual, including constant hair shampooing, was not advocated (or practical) since water had to be hauled and heated.

While much personal cleansing took place in the kitchen, especially in cold weather so one could strip near the heat source, the bedroom too had furniture which served in a bathroom substitute capacity. In the 1800s small three or four drawer chests (obsolete catalogs call these bureau commodes) frequently featured a retractable rod which could be pulled out to hold towels, or there were types with towel bars at each end. Others, dubbed commode washstands, had various numbers of drawers and a one or two door cupboard area where washing supplies were stored. Some included towel rods. Families could arrange their toilet sets with basins, cold and hot water pitchers, toothbrush holders, and soap dishes on top if they desired. The matching slop jar, modest or ornate, had a handle so that waste could be carried outside to be discarded. The pot for nocturnal relief usually peeked shyly and demurely from beneath the bed.

Today the past's rustic lift-top commode, at times with a fake drawer, may show black water rings deeply staining the wood which indicate that the pitcher was placed in the lower well and the bowl on the raised sections while they were still dripping wet.

Above: Washstand, pine and poplar. Size: 21½" wide, 16" deep, 35" high.
$165.00 - 185.00

Right: Bureau washstand with towel bar ends, pine and poplar, artificially grained and stencilled. Size: 27" wide, 16" deep, 29" high.
$235.00 - 255.00

Lift top commode, walnut, plank sides, right hand drawer is a fake. Size: 36½" wide, 18½" deep, 34¾" high.

$345.00 - 385.00

Washstand, pine, hole in top to accommodate bowl, walnut wooden knob on lower drawer. Size: 14½" wide, 14½" deep, 28½" high.

$165.00 - 190.00

Commode washstand, pine, mismatched knobs. Size: 30" wide, 15" deep, 29" high.

$225.00 - 250.00

The common washstand usually included towel bars and had a table-top, a drawer, plus a bottom exposed shelf for holding the grooming aids. Since it was an open arrangement, it was less expensive than the cupboard or the drawer varieties. Another type of wooden washstand had a hole in the top so the base of a bowl, either metal or ceramic, could be sunk into it. Some, triangular in shape, fit into corners. (More pictures are included under bedrooms.) These quaint obsolete furnishings are being beckoned back to appear in modern homes, their traditional purposes ignored, since they function as servers in dining rooms, as end tables in "parlors," or for storage most anywhere. They're versatile as are their commode counterparts.

When plumbing brought water cascading in and draining out, people seeking to be up-to-date discarded the items bathrooms and kitchen sinks displaced, at times relegating them to the basement, barn, shed, or attic. Some, utilized as is, substituted as tool holders, food containers, or porch storage units. Others were painted, sawed, hacked, or converted by removing such parts as backs or towel rods to fit a designated space, or to meet a new purpose. Many perished. Survivors are being sought, scrounged up for social service once again.

As every housekeeper knows, a kitchen requires work space. By definition, a dry sink is a cabinet with an open tray top which is usually lined with zinc. It is said the slurring of the word "zinc" yields the modern term "sink," and since water had to be carried in from the well, this kitchen piece was indeed dry in itself. Perhaps there was a drainage hole in the bottom middle of the tray which permitted waste liquid to flow down into a bucket beneath, from whence it could be extracted to empty. Here kitchen tasks which required the use of water could be performed and splashes would not leak onto the floor or damage a wooden surface. There were great variations in dry sinks because some had shelves above the zinc, and some included pull-out cutting boards. A Pennsylvania type featured a breadboard hinged cover which provided a space where loaves of bread could be kneaded and shaped when it was pulled down to cover the hollow well. Small, large, plain, or carved, wainscoted — most sinks were made of pine or poplar and occasionally oak, chestnut, walnut, or cherry with combinations of woods possible. They enhance today's country kitchens, and with the prevalence of plants in decors at present, they can become vases of greenery. Many times the zinc has deteriorated and has to be removed so that either the plain boards are permitted to show or, with additional expense, a costly copper lining is inserted. Some people apply adhesive backed paper to cover the tray in a colorful, low-in-price manner.

Dry sink, pine, wainscoted ends, pull out cutting board is scooped out from repeated usage, back rail with one shelf. Size: 52" wide, 22" deep, 44" high.

$400.00 - 450.00

Primitive water or bucket benches were frequent occupants on side or back porches or in small utility entrances. Here hired hands bent over a basin and sloshed water on their hands and faces before they entered the house to join the family for the "noonday" meal. There were also rough cabinets where buckets and basins were weathered by Mother Nature's stern hands or blackened by penetrating water. They were designed for serviceable tough treatment, not eye pleasure.

Modern women applaud the technology that produced automatic washers and throw in a load at any time they desire, occupying themselves elsewhere as the machine wets, whisks, and whirls the wash. This was not true years ago. Traditionally, the family wash was done by hand on Monday. Some affluent families had wash rooms where garments were scrubbed or outbuildings where the laundry was done, but the impecunious ones worked in the kitchen, or during summer's heat, outside. Tubs were placed on benches and filled with water warmed on a wood burning stove or dipped from a giant kettle hung in the

Above: Water bench, pine; the sides, top and bottom are one piece boards, square nails. Size: 48" wide, 17½" deep, 27" high.
$95.00 - 110.00

Right: Dry sink, pine, original zinc lining, two small drawers with porcelain knobs. Size: 44" wide, 21" deep, 35" high.
$375.00 - 410.00

fireplace or over an outdoor flame. It was hard, backaching work for a woman to massage yellowish harsh soap (often made from fats hoarded in the family kitchen) into dirty garments and rub-a-dub them up and down on a scrub board to get them clean before she rinsed and wrung them out by twisting them in her hands and placed them to dry over fences, spread flat on the grass, or hung on lines strung between posts, trees, or buildings.

Drying presented a problem in inclement weather, even for Abigial Adams, wife of John Adams, the second president and the first one to live in the then uncompleted White House. Swampy grounds, not a yard, surrounded the mansion in 1800, causing the First Lady to write to her daughter, ". . . the great unfinished audience room (now the East Room) I make a drying-room of, to hang up clothes in. . ."

In remote valleys of the Appalachian Mountains women still toil to tote water from springs bubbling up in pools out of the ground, heat it, and scrub clothes much as pioneer women did in days of yore before push-bottom machines evolved. No one knows who wrote this advice, but one can visualize a diminutive, wizened, granny-type lady in a long dress with long sleeves, a sun bonnet on her wispy hair, her gnarled hands holding a molded stick as she stirs garments in a blackened, almost witch-caldron-type kettle over an outdoor bonfire. She serves with a glad heart, perhaps filled with thoughts of love for each family member whose clothes she is cleansing. Here are instructions such an anonymous laborer left for posterity.

Receet for Washing Clothes
Anonymous

1. bild fire in backyard to het kettle of rain water.

2. Set tubs so smoke won't blow in eyes if wind is pert.

3. shave one hol cake lie sope in bilin water.

4. sort things, make 3 piles
   1 pile white, 1 pile cullord,
   1 pile werk britches and rags.

5. stir flour in cold water to smooth, then thin down with bilin water.

6. rub dirty spots on board, scrub hard. then bile. rub cullord but don't bile — just rench and starch.

7. take white things out of kettle with broomstick handel. then rench, blew and starch.

8. spread tee towels on grass.

9. hang old rags on fence.

10. pore rench water in flower bed.

11. scrub porch with hot sopy water.

12. turn tubs upside down.

13. go put on cleen dress — smooth hair with side combs. brew cup of tea and rest and rock a spell and count blessings.

Rocking chair, rush seat, hickory, maple, oak. Size: 14½" to seat, 36" high.

$120.00 - 150.00

What a beautiful woman that recipe writer was!

Today's homemakers like wash day relics despite their torturing work record. Corrugated scrub boards, with their parallel ridges and grooves, are hung to receive magnet-applied family bulletins, appear as humorous kitchen band "musical instruments," or four may be attached together to form a planter. As time progressed, hand cranked wringers on stands were developed, and these now serve as tables or provide a green haven for plants. Benches, which once held tubs, hug fireplaces, are seats around kitchen and picnic tables, or become coffee and bedside tables. When clothes were "biled" (boiled), scalding could occur easily, and tongs helped remove hot dripping garments from the heated water. Today the boilers, iron, tin, or copper, are beauty aids with potted geraniums in them, form magazine racks, or become fireplace accessories while tongs and stirrers are wall hangings. Washers offered in late 1800, early 1900 mail order catalogues are store props, beverage units, flower containers, or hampers. Originally, slightly misleading ads declared a child could manage these cumbersome hand-operated machines (but now this is actually possible with the modern twist-a-dial settings).

Ingenuity is required to reinstate castoffs in contemporary homes where interest is focused on a backward glance. Ignore old timers who had to use primitives in their youth and who shake their heads in disdain and disgust that such lowly articles have switched to become popular parlor pieces. If they please you, accept with affection attractive Americana rustics since "do your own thing" decorating demands the dramatic.

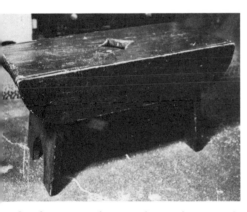

Stool, pine, similar in style to a larger wash bench, old red paint. Size: 24" wide, 11" deep, 14" high.
$65.00 - 85.00

Waterbench, pine. Size: 30" wide, 17¼" deep, 28" high.
$140.00 - 165.00

Commode washstand, pine, projection drawer, wooden knobs. Size: 30″ wide, 15″ deep, 29″ high.
$195.00 - 225.00

Dry sink, pine, Scandinavian origin. Size: 27¾″ wide, 15¾″ deep at well, 43″ high.

$325.00 - 375.00

Dry sink, pine and poplar. Size: 48" wide, 17" deep, 48" high.

$350.00 - 400.00

Dry sink, pine and poplar, hutch style, one board doors. Size: 39" wide, 16" deep, 51" high.

$365.00 - 400.00

Dry sink, pine mortise and tenon and pegged doors. Size: 43″ wide, 17½″ deep, 29½″ high.

$275.00 - 350.00

Dry sink, pine and poplar, tin lined sink projects over base. Size: 56″ wide, 25″ deep at well, 34″ high.

$400.00 - 450.00

Dry sink, pine, one piece sides, dove-tailed drawers. Size: 47″ wide, 18¼″ deep, 48½″ high.

$325.00 - 350.00

Dry sink, pine and poplar, replaced door catches. Size: 42″ wide, 17¾″ deep, 40″ high.

$300.00 - 350.00

Lift top commode, ash. Size: 29″ wide, 16″ deep, 30″ high.

$225.00 - 250.00

Washstand, poplar and cherry. Size: 32″ wide, 16″ deep, 31″ high. $195.00 - 225.00

Commode washstand, pine, drawer and door at each end, ball type feet. Size: 38″ wide, 16″ deep, 29″ high.

$375.00 - 450.00

Dry sink, pine, two different size drawers, finger insert opening holes instead of knobs on doors. Size: 48″ wide, 18½″ deep, 42½″ high.

$400.00 - 475.00

Chapter 4
Kitchen Capers

A young couple recently rejuvenated a sagging deserted farm house, and the main entrance into their hospitable home is through the expansive kitchen with its heat emitting, pot bellied, cast metal stove. A creaky creeping rocker and low-backed chairs, seemingly meant for tilting against the wall, invite a person to come set a spell as odors of home baking waft from a modern oven. The host and hostess proudly state, "This is the room in which we do most of our entertaining. If we try to sit somewhere else, people seem to gravitate back here. After all, the kitchen with its warmth was traditionally the center of the farm family's home, and we're harboring that habit."

But it wasn't simply the warm stove which drew the family together around it on cold wintry nights. Mama was the magnetic force that united all. Mama spent untotaled hours directing the kitchen task force which could include daughters, perhaps a hired girl, and a maiden or widowed aunt who, in those more sheltered days, might not have a means of support since female education was not stressed and teaching or sewing were the most common professions for women. Customarily there was a kitchen garden near the door where lettuce, tomatoes, peas, beans, berries, onions, corn, cabbages, cucumbers, and other fresh produce for table use and to preserve for winter's needs were grown. Mama's "butter 'n egg" money was earned from the sale of extra eggs she gathered from the

Above: Plank seat chair, maple and poplar, used in kitchen.

$60.00 - 75.00

Left: Splat back, plank seat rocker, maple, ash, pine. Size: seat 12¾" from floor, 37½" tall. $125.00 - 150.00

nests of the flock of chickens she kept and from the sale of butter she churned from the rich cream skimmed off the top of the milk the family cows gave. Traditionally the butter was hers to do with as she desired. She might pack the sweet, firm yellow butter in tubs covered with clean cloths, or it could be shaped into pound rectangles or rounds with molds, including ones with attractive geometric, fruit, nut, grain, flower, animal, or fowl designs.

The aroma in the kitchen was always enticing, but especially so in summer and autumn when, as vegetables and fruits ripened, they were processed for later consumption. Fruits were washed and picked over to be boiled and bubbled with sugar to make jellies and jams. Small jelly cupboards held these shimmering red, black, purple, and orange preserves or tangy brown apple butter taste treats.

Frequently, each family unit baked its own bread. These homemade fruit spreads plus the newly churned butter were especially tempting when combined with crusty loaves fresh from the oven. Before commercial yeast was available, housewives made their own with a batter of potato water, sugar, salt, and flour left uncovered for several hours. Yeasts, among the simplest type of plants, float in the air, increasing very rapidly, and when the proper type suitable for bread-making lodged in the batter, it served as a leavening agent to make the dough rise high and light. A small portion of successfully fermented dough might be saved each time as a starter for new batches for bread baking. Therefore, some kind of container for dough was essential in most homes.

Quantities could be mixed and allowed to rise in dough troughs, trays, or bowls, early examples of which were carved out of a section of a tree limb, and the rough marks of the hand work become evident by running the hands across the surface to feel the undulations or by an eye inspection to note imperfections.

Above: Butter churn, pine and poplar. Size: 14" across handle end, 12" deep, 13" high.

$135.00 - 150.00

Left: Butter churn, oak, plunger moves up and down and has round holes in round disk at bottom of long handle. Size: 5¾" to 8½" diameter from bottom to top.

$130.00 - 155.00

Dough box, pine and poplar. Size: 39¼" wide, 19¼" deep, 26½" high.
$225.00 - 275.00

Dough box, poplar, portable, dovetailed corners. Size:
27½" wide, 15" deep, 10" high.
$125.00 - 150.00

Jelly cupboard, cherry. Size: 33¼" wide, 17½" deep,
40¾" tall.

$200.00 - 250.00

Dough boxes were more sophisticated, especially of the tote-about type with handles on the sides so they could be lifted onto a table when ingredients were being mixed or kneaded. An easy way to fashion these containers was to fasten six wide boards together, one for the top, one for the bottom, and four for the sides, hence the name six board chest. A butt joint was simple to use, and many were made with this type of construction. Dovetailed versions are in abundance also. Dough boxes could have removable lids which tended to be reversible so that they could be set in to fit securely in place or could have their brace cross pieces upright and showing. Other versions were self contained units sitting on splayed leg bases (canted, slanted out legs).

It is not uncommon to find that legs have been attached to a portable dough box so that it could function as a table. Some are available with a red milk base paint on them, a true treasure to the purist.

Wooden bowl, pine, hand crafted from part of a log. Size: 37″ wide, 17″ deep, 6″ high.
$125.00 - 150.00

Dough box, poplar, legs splayed, turned, and pegged to apron, large overhanging lid. Size: 43½″ wide, 21½″ deep, 28″ high.
$335.00 - 385.00

Just as the breads were homemade, so were the desserts. With the prevalence of berries and fruits (wild varieties abounded) pies were popular, and many might be made at once, either for prompt consumption by a large family, or in an area where winter brought continuous freezing temperatures, to be frozen for future needs in an unheated attic storage area by nature's own extreme cold. Since free-loading rodents enjoyed pastries, a special cupboard or "pie safe" was designed to discourage their gnawing presence and to permit air to circulate to help retard molding. These case pieces with their shelves where baked articles could be kept "safe" (hence, "pie safe") contained tin or zinc sheets which were punched with attractive designs on the door and side panels. These made them impervious to sharp animal teeth and the disease spreading fly. Perforated geometric patterns including circles and stars were among the more common decorations created by the series of tiny holes or slots which pierced the metal, but more elaborate designs such as buildings or simple scenes do exist. People ask whether the designs were punched in or out. The displaced rough edges of some pierced details face inside and some protrude to the outside so the answer is either. As time passed, it was possible to purchase replacement metal sheets for rusted out or damaged pie safes. At times the tin was replaced by screening or glass. Punched board panels were a later development.

Pie safe, walnut, plank sides, flower designs in pierced tin. Size: 35" wide, 14" deep, 54" high.
$285.00 - 325.00

Pie safe, star and heart design in tin panels, plank sides. Size: 41" wide, 15" deep, 54" high.
$245.00 - 285.00

Generally, the frames were of pine or poplar, but there are hardwood examples available. When the corner posts extended above the wooden top and had holes drilled in them, the cupboard could be laced with ropes and suspended from the ceiling well above the damp cellar floor, and this became a hanging pie safe. These are not so common as the standing variety and are frequently Pennsylvanian in origin.

Since baking was a home occupation, meal, grain, or flour chests were prevalent kitchen equipment. Some of these lift tops had various compartments where the different types of bread-making fundamental ingredients were stored because, in addition to wheat, much rye and corn meal helped feed the self-sufficient family. More frequent than the multi-units were single slant-top bins where large supplies of flour were kept. In this era, before today's mixes and instant meals, homemade goodies pampered the palate, and a large container was essential to hold sugar. Wooden buckets with lids or barrels held the "store-bought" variety. Until Civil War times (1861-1865), refined sugar was molded into loaves and cones and had to be cut with sugar shears or pulverized with a hammer before it was incorporated into a recipe. In fact, a gracious hostess might dangle a generous lump on a string from the ceiling when she entertained at tea so that it could be swung from guest to guest and each one could nibble some of the sweetener as it passed. Families used maple sugar, honey, and molasses as sweetening agents, and it was not until almost 1870 that granulated sugar gained popularity. Despite this, grocers had to employ special augers to loosen the hardened sugar in barrels and had to grind it before it could be sold.

Dough cabinet, pine, two bins, three drawers, top folds to each side for extended work area. Size: 37" wide, (74" wide extended), 18" deep, 37" high.
$375.00 - 425.00

Hanging pie safe, Pennsylvania Dutch, one sheet tin pierced panels on sides and front, mortise and tenon joints, pegged construction, hand planed. Size: 36" wide, 19" deep, 35" high.
$650.00 - $700.00

Salt was needed also, and it is found underground, but sometimes it is near or above the surface and frontiersmen were always glad to locate a salt lick, as it was called. Small wall boxes of wood were made to hold this seasoning.

Because breakable, hard-to-transport, expensive glass and china were rare items on the frontier, homemade wooden utensils predominated. Naturally, the male members fashioned most of this treenware (small wooden objects, the word itself derived from "tree"). Such plates, bowls, butter paddles, buckets, skimmers, spoons, spinning wheels, or other essentials ranged from crude to those artistically decorated, depending on the skill and patience of the maker. There was a cluttered appearance to the food preparing area in the very early days when the room was small and a fireplace had the trifold purpose of providing for warmth, light, and cooking. Iron or copper or brass pots cluttered the hearth. Wooden bowls, paddles, spoons, churns sat companionably about, perhaps with grinders, graters, or mortars (bowl) and pestles (pounders) near, since spices and sugars came in whole form and chunks and had to be pulverized before they could be utilized. Dried herbs and onions dangled from pegs, and shelves on the wall sufficed when the family's supplies were meager. A gradual evolutionary process transformed a series of unrelated shelves into a case piece when they were united with a box structure surrounding them to form a plain cupboard. Later panels and cornices and feet became attractive additions.

Flour box, pine, hinged top slants to front from rear. Size: 22″ wide, 16″ deep, 29½″ high.
$95.00 - 125.00

Mortar and pestle, burn mark at top edge, incised line around bowl. Size: 5½" diameter, 6" high. Pestle 9" high.

$65.00 - 85.00

Spinning wheel, oak, signed by maker, Troxell. Size: 24" wide, 30½" high.

$275.00 - 300.00

Sugar bucket, pine. Size: 14½" diameter, 13¼" high.

$65.00 - 90.00

A combination of exposed top shelves with an enclosed base frequently was referred to as a "dresser" and those originating in Wales acquired the title "Welsh dresser" as did similar styles made elsewhere. Drawers might be included and straight outlines gradually changed as scallops were cut into the side supports and shelves or other decorative details were added. Triangular versions backed into the space where two walls meet became known as corner cupboards, either free-standing or built-in.

Furnishings of these types became necessary as pewter and pottery began to replace wooden plates in homes and had to be kept somewhere. Rails held plates erect or later, straight grooves were incised into shelves to help prevent displayed wares from slipping by inserting them into the slot and permitting them to recline against the back of the piece. A "pewter cupboard" with open shelves at the top traditionally was used to show these articles made from an alloy of tin and other metals such as copper, and/or antimony, lead, or bismuth. Crude frontier style

Pewter hutch, pine, one piece, H hinges on door. Size: 43" wide, 14" deep, 72" high.

$950.00 - 1,000.00

Corner cupboard, pine, scalloped shelves, molded cornice, H hinges on door. Size: 34" wide, 16" deep, 74" high.

$900.00 - 950.00

homes lacked many of these refinements because people couldn't carry large furnishings as they migrated westward in their horse or oxen drawn wagons, aboard river rafts, or as they pushed westward on foot, perhaps pulling handcarts. Families might be forced to abandon unnecessary excesses en route to homestead new areas when they crossed mountains, streams, deserts, or ran from Indians on the westward trail. A farmer craftsman could complete a cupboard for his wife only after essential home building, farming, and hunting tasks were under control. Of course, country cabinetmakers and carpenters produced them also.

By the late 1830s, a mechanical plunger was developed to press glass into molds so that more items could be turned out than when glass was blown by human lung power; and when cheaper ingredients appeared in the formula, the common person could afford to buy glass. Porcelain products gained ground as the 1800s waned and so china cabinets for storage and display developed. Some of these, while perhaps factory made, retain a humble country air.

Kitchen cupboard, circa 1900, poplar, ash, maple, one piece. Size: 36½" wide, 16½" deep, 72" high.

$245.00 - 275.00

Chimney cupboard, pine. This type of cupboard was built in the wall by the chimney to store pots, pans, and other essentials. Size: 24" wide, 19½" deep, 76½" high.

$350.00 - 400.00

Now homemakers are seeking manufactured cabinets their grandmothers or great-grandmothers discarded in favor of built-ins. These cabinets date to the early decades of the 1900s with spacious pull out bins for flour and sugar plus drawers in the bases, a top work area, and shelves above. Some had a swing out flour sifter attachment and a retractable breadboard, as added surface for rolling pies, punching dough, or cutting and chopping. A company in Indiana, the Hoosier State, turned out many of these helpful units so the generic term "Hoosier Cabinet" is often applied to them. These are late rustics that moderns have adopted, sometimes returning them to kitchen duty, sometimes removing the bins to form a desk while retaining the inserts as waste receptacles. An advertisement in *The Madison Daily Herald*, published in Madison, Indiana, Tuesday, June 21, 1910, shouts the virtues of this kitchen piece.

<hr>

YOU'VE GOT IT TO DO

Wife needs a helper with the work; you can't get a good
girl; you've tried it; listen, here's a secret: it's just like play with a

HOOSIER KITCHEN CABINET

YOU DON'T have to feed it, or house it, or teach it, or
wage it or beau it. The Hoosier is it; everything
handy, ready to use; sit down and stay
WITH it; saves steps, saves time, saves expenses.
Say, she's a dear, and you know it. She ought to have
it. Don't wait to be coaxed, get it for her now.

**
VAIL'S

<hr>

Doesn't this ad make you want to join the buyer crunch? (Providing you can find a Hoosier Cabinet or its counterpart, that is.) Buyers want them even though they don't meet the U.S. government qualifications for an antique. It's similar to the "Baby Sister Blues" of the 1920s era as a girl wails that she is "just too young to go out with boys; just too old to play with toys." These kitchen pieces are "just too young to be antique; not a hundred nor quite unique" yet they are no longer designated "kitchen only" but can creep into a country-type modern setting with ease. Seeking new uses for old timers seems to be part of the enchantment associated with retrieving them.

Closed cupboard, two piece, walnut. Size: 43½" wide, 18½" deep at base, 81" high.

$650.00 - 750.00

One piece closed cupboard, pine, pegged doors, one board plank sides. Size: 41" wide, 17" deep, 81" high.

$650.00 - 700.00

Countertop cupboard, pine. Size: 26" wide, 12" deep, 38" high.

$225.00 - 250.00

Jelly cupboard (kitchen press), pine, pegged doors, plank ends. Size: 41″ wide, 15½″ deep, 54½″ high.

$250.00 - 300.00

Two piece closed cupboard, pine. Size: 46″ wide, 21½″ deep, 76″ high.

$550.00 - 600.00

Jelly cupboard, maple, pegged doors, plank ends. Size: 48″ wide, 20″ deep, 66″ high.
$400.00 - 450.00

Jelly cupboard, pine. Size: 42" wide, 16" deep, 53" high.
$200.00 - 250.00

Kitchen cupboard, pine, one piece. Size: 39" wide, 18¼" deep at base, 74½" high.

$450.00 - 500.00

Closed cupboard, maple, poplar, New England origin, 18th century. Size: 55" wide, 20" deep, 81½" high.
$650.00 - 700.00

Above: Kitchen cabinet, maple, one piece. Size: 37" wide, 15¼" deep, 71" high.

$175.00 - 225.00

Above right: Corner cupboard, walnut, one piece. Size: 52" wide, 18" deep, 82" high.

$1,350.00 - 1,450.00

Right: Corner cupboard, pine, two pieces. Size: 61" wide at base, 32" deep, 68" high.

$550.00 - 600.00

Corner cupboard, cherry, one piece. Size: 45″ wide, 20″ deep, 85″ high.

$895.00 - 945.00

Corner cupboard, two pieces, cherry. Size: 42″ wide at base, 20″ deep, 70″ high.

$600.00 - 650.00

One piece closed cupboard, pine. Size: 38″ wide, 18″ deep, 64½″ high.

$400.00 - 475.00

Two piece pie shelf cupboard, poplar, maple, butternut. Size: 45″ wide, 18″ deep, 82″ high.

$745.00 - 795.00

Sideboard chest, pine. Size: 38″ wide, 20″ deep, 32″ high.

$275.00 - 325.00

Two piece closed cupboard, walnut. Size: 45" wide, 18" deep, 76" high.

$600.00 - 700.00

Kitchen cupboard, butternut and ash, glass panels replace wooden ones, vent hole on each side near base. Size: 39" wide, 14½" deep, 70" high.

$275.00 - 325.00

Hanging cupboard, maple. Size: 30" wide, 9½" deep, 34" high.

$175.00 - 225.00

Above: Pie safe, chestnut, pierced star designs in circle on tin panels. Size: 40″ wide, 15½″ deep, 62½″ high.

$325.00 - 350.00

Above right: Pie safe, poplar, pierced tin on sides too. Size: 38″ wide, 16″ deep, 61″ high.

$245.00 - 275.00

Right: Pie safe, pine, screen panels. Size: 31″ wide, 15½″ deep, 44″ high.

$165.00 - 185.00

Closed cupboard, ash, chestnut, maple, one piece. Size: 37" wide, 15" deep, 69" high. Label on back reads: "Sink Cases, Schwartz Mfg. Co., Plymouth, Wisconsin."
$375.00 - 400.00

Closed cupboard, mixed light woods, one piece. Size: 37" wide, 15½" deep, 70½" high.
$225.00 - 250.00

Jelly cupboard, pine, wooden panels have been replaced by glass ones. Size: 39½" wide, 15½" deep, 64" high.
$275.00 - 325.00

Corner cupboard, poplar, open top, two pieces. Size: 48" wide, 74" high.

$450.00 - 500.00

Open cupboard, poplar, two pieces probably not originally together (a marriage). Size: 41½" wide, 18" deep, 70½" high.

$475.00 - 500.00

Hanging corner cupboard, pine. Size: 23½" wide, 30½" high.

$190.00 - 220.00

Hanging shelf, pine, shelves graduated from 7", 8", 8½" and 10", incised plate ridges in shelves. Size: 34" wide, 9" deep, 44" high.

$165.00 - 190.00

Hanging shelf, pine, scalloped edges. Size: 28" wide, 8¾" deep, 31" high.

$155.00 - 185.00

Hanging spice cabinet, porcelain markers, maple. Size: 12″ wide, 6″ deep, 26″ high.
$175.00 - 200.00

Water bench cupboard, pine. Size: 28¼″ wide, 16½″ deep, 29½″ high.
$135.00 - 165.00

Sideboard, walnut, three recessed drawers at top. Size: 53″ wide, 20½″ deep, 44″ high.
$350.00 - 375.00

Sideboard, pine, walnut knobs on top drawers. Size: 48″ wide, 19½″ deep, 34½″ high.
$350.00 - 425.00

Grain bin, top lifts up, pine. Size: 43″ wide, 25″ deep, 40″ high.
$395.00 - 425.00

Flour bin, pine, hinged top lifts. Size: 26½" wide, 17" deep, 27½" high.
$135.00 - 155.00

Bowl, butternut. Size: 35" wide, 10½" deep, 5½" high. $85.00 - 100.00

Mortar and pestle, maple, traces of blue paint remain. Size: 8″ high, 4½″ diameter. Pestle – 10½″.

$65.00 - 75.00

Coffee grinder, pine, original label, Arcade Manufacturing Company.

$55.00 - 65.00

Wine press, oak. Size: 18″ high, 9″ diameter.
$65.00 - 75.00

Pipe box, false drawer. Size: 5" wide, 5¼" deep, 17" high.

$75.00 - 95.00

Spoon rack, four holes in top shelf, three holes in lower shelf. Size: 11¾" wide, 6" deep, 18" high.

$75.00 - 95.00

Scoop and mallet. Scoop is a hand crafted butternut reproduction. Size: 13½" wide, 10½" diameter.

$55.00

Mallet is 11" long and incised with V.A. McGuigan.

$8.50

Spinning wheel, small flax type, oak, maple, walnut. Wheel 20" in diameter, 54" peak height.

$275.00 - 300.00

Child's room, featuring pine kitchen cupboard, 37½" high (**$115.00**), ice cream table and two chairs with spectacle backs (**$150.00 the set**), soft maple doll's highchair (**$55.00**), and wicker doll cradle (**$35.00**).

Maple cannonball finial rope bed. **$500.00**

Pine three legged tavern-type table with triangular lower shelf.   **$225.00**

Windsor comb-back highchair, splayed legs.   **$125.00**

Cherry refectory table, breadboard ends.   **$800.00**

Cupboard, ash with poplar sides. $325.00

Bentwood butter churn with porcelain knobbed lift top. $175.00

Oak Boone Kitchen Cupboard, made in Lebanon, Indiana with frosted glass doors, circa 1910. This type cabinet was often called a Hoosier cabinet.
$325.00

Pine store flour or coffee box, slant hinged lid, one piece boards 20" wide used on each end.
$125.00

Above: Maple child's rope bed that has had board inserted to form coffee table. Size: 40¼″ long, 23″ wide, 24″ high.

$500.00

Pine, slant, lift lid desk ($250.00), pine hanging corner cupboard ($115.00), pine hanging newspaper pocket ($60.00), and cranberry scoop ($150.00).

Pine dough tray with ends made from one piece of wood forming bootjack type legs. Two compartments inside.

$250.00

Butternut dry sink, tongue and groove framed doors, square nails.

$375.00

Poplar dry sink with cupboard top, zinc lined. $750.00

Pine wing back chair with drawer at base for Bible, circa 1750. Museum quality.

Maple top, walnut base round tavern-type table, 36″ in diameter.
$175.00
Pine butter churn, 21½″ tall, all original.
$175.00

Cherry fall front table top desk, two pieces with top, above pigeon holes, that lifts for a storage compartment.
$750.00

Chapter 5
Ladies and Gentlemen, Please Be Seated

"Come set a spell" is a rustic hospitable invitation, and in pioneer homes, benches and stools were the norm since the home handyman could construct them with accessible tools without excessive difficulty. Simplicity keynoted a log split in half and flattened on top with stick-like legs protruding from the rounded bottom. Likewise, rough tables could be formed in this manner with the bark remaining on the under portion.

There are benches consisting of a top and two boards, one at each side, for legs. When an upside down "V" was cut in the board ends, the result reminded people of a bootjack (a frame which was placed on the floor so a man could wedge his heel in the "V" and yank to pull off his high boots easier). This construction became known as a "bootjack leg." If a small hand grip slot were cut in the top, it added to the portable qualities.

Benches not merely for sitting were work surfaces with a drawer to hold tools or a top which lifted to make a storage space available. In a day when people home-repaired their own shoes, a small bench with such a feature helped keep supplies handy. Of course, various occupations had specific benches as working units, as for example, one on which a cobbler cut leather and hammered to tap boots.

Bench, pine, bootjack legs. Size: 22½" wide, 9" deep, 15½" high.
$75.00 - 90.00

A fancier style had a back with spindles from the seat to a top rail. A specialized, hard-to-acquire rocking variation had a section with a front rail behind which a baby could be placed so that the wee one would not roll off. The mother could sit on the portion with no protecting guard and sew or perform other required tasks as she watched baby and swayed gently backward and forward. The common name for these baby tenders is "mammy bench."

During the early development of this country, the lack of central heating caused people to huddle close to the open fireplace on blustery winter days. Because of the prevailing drafts, the idea of the settle bench evolved. With its all wooden back and wide wings, it kept the cold off the sitters' backs and heads while the leaping colorful flames of the burning logs toasted them in front.

One deviating space saver slips in and out of various names much as it adjusts to different postures and uses. The chair (for one person), hutch, or settle table (for two or more sitters) is a versatile convertible which comes in various forms. Its top can be round or rectangular, large or small. Behold, now it's a chair.

Settle bench, pine and maple, lift seat storage area. Size: 54" wide, 16½" deep, 49" high.
$895.00 - 925.00

Presto chango, flip the flat tall back down to rest on the arms, insert pegs to hold it steady, and there's a table. If the bench seat has hinges, lift the lid and there's a place to stash away articles, or a drawer may be present. Now how's that for a compact, utilitarian furnishing? Combination chair-tables, available in the colonial period, were copied by craftsmen of the 1800s, and current factories produce what they term "Early American" settle tables, but check for wide thick boards of varying sizes and other signs of passe' construction as listed in chapter two if you seek a vintage article.

Since people usually were shorter, tables frequently tended to be likewise, or had deep aprons (horizontal strips of wood covering the legs where they join the top) which disturb today's tall sitters who need more stretching space. At the courthouse in Metamora, Illinois, lawyer Abraham Lincoln could not get his lanky Yankee legs underneath the table. If it were raised to accommodate him, shorter colleagues would have problems. The solution — a section of the apron was cut away to meet the Honest Abe knee needs for more space, and current buyers of antiques have to be aware of this problem, if they expect to serve tall people.

Hutch or settle table, pine, late eighteenth century. Size: Top – 56" wide, 39" deep; Base – 48" wide, 18" to seat.

$1,200.00 - 1,300.00

There are exceptions, but large tables were not the rule in the 1700s. If a crowd came to dine, plank tops could be placed over horses or trestles, and later tables were made with such bases and called "trestle tables." There were gate legs which swung out to support raised drop leaves, the sweeping motion which was similar to that of a fence gate, providing the name. Other drop leaf forms were available, rectangular, oval, or round, and were fashioned from various native woods.

In grand homes of the late 1700s to early 1800s, a series of tables could be pushed together to form a large dining space. These "banquet boards" might consist of a central unit or perhaps two with rectangular drop leaves which could be held in the up position when a wooden support or an extra leg was properly positioned. Two semi-circular side tables might have an oblong attached leaf and could be added at each end to form one long surface. These components matched in height, wood, leg style, and were meant to be side-by-side companions when needed. In a humbler home, tables which were not compatible could be pushed together as required, and imagine the problems presented when they varied in tallness or width; but amidst jovial festivities, probably no one cared.

Pedestal tables, both large and small, proved popular. Housewives of the mid-1800s must have been delighted when extension tables with additional portable leaves which could be inserted gained acclaim. Now one unit, either oval or squarish, could be made small for family or increased leaf by leaf for company. It was a practical invention.

Since rooms in early backwoods homes were usually small and the main room had to serve a variety of functions, tables which could be dismantled, converted into chairs, or had space saving drop leaves were desirable. Country areas liked the harvest table which was long yet sparse in width with a narrow rectangular drop leaf or two which could be supported by pull-out wooden slides. Some had drawers in the ends. Cabinetmakers selected forest woods, and since pine was 'most everywhere, and easy to work, it was frequently utilized. Poplar, oak, hickory, cherry, and walnut were readily available. The picturesque name recalls the gleaning season at summer's end when pumpkins, corn, beans, squash, apples, peaches, pears, grapes, and plums offered culinary delights.

Harvest table, pine top, maple legs. Size: 67" wide, 47½" deep with leaves up, 27½" high.
$625.00 - 700.00

Many years ago, monks ate at long, narrow tables, often made of carved oak and heavy in appearance. The stretchers were close to the floor and gave a solid appearance to the structure. The dining rooms were refectories so the non-extendable tables where the cloistered brethern ate were called refectory tables. Sometime during the sixteenth century, Italian, English, and French designers added a double-top extension to form a draw, drawing, drawer, draw-out, or draw-top table. Terminal leaves could be drawn out and pulled up level with the table surface when in use or folded back or pushed down and under the main section when not needed. Designs could vary because the table top itself could sink to be on par with the level of the leaves. Ordinarily a ponderous base helped provide the good balance that was essential when the extended leaves added weight at the ends. And, it is said, a refectory-type table had an added advantage because it could be used to sleep upon if the need arose. When winter was raging and raw, the floor was hard-packed dirt with the fire slowly sinking in the fireplace at night, and a chink or two between the log walls was not plugged sufficiently but let in a whistle of wind, cold, or even snow, a spare table-top bed might look inviting if sleeping quarters were needed. Sounds good, but chances that a log cabin resident would own such a table are minimal.

Other tables include ones for lamps, kitchen needs, parlor types, or whatever families required. Small one- or two-drawer stands were multi-purpose and useful almost anywhere, doing bedside duty, serving in the living room to hold clutter, or for work tables such as sewers use. Tilt-tops with a hinge device so that the top can fold down to a vertical position on the base to save space, can be rustic, but normally, these were elegant in nature, reserved for tea time service in elaborate settings.

Windsor Chairs

As has been shown, benches were the norm in humble homes and could be pulled up to tables with ease at meal times. If a pioneer family owned one chair for an elderly person to sit on or for a guest to rest upon, that was luxury. The Windsor chair, an English immigrant to the United States around 1725, can be country-ish or citified and is characterized by many gracefully shaped stick-like spokes (spindles) in the back. Antique authorities label fictitious the romantic tale which links the Windsor chair to King George III, England's ruler from 1760-1820. Supposedly, this monarch sought shelter in a rustic cottage during a storm and found the furniture compatible to his corpulent torso so he ordered similar seats for Windsor Castle, thus giving them their name. This disagrees with their earlier introduction date to the American colonies and with advertisements that precede George by at least half a century, so many feel the chairs probably are named for the market town, not the palace, and there are those who claim the design goes back centuries earlier.

English versions appear masculine with heavier lines which utilize a pierced splat in the back, and the legs are at the edge of the seat creating a stiff, straight appearance. Those of American heritage are refined and gentled with a many-spindled (at least 7 or 9 in old ones) construction. These required subtle skill to fashion because these "sticks," carefully shaped for comfort, varied in length, diminishing in size when they tapered from the center to the sides on various styles. Frequently, unseasoned wood which shrank as it dried gripped the seasoned spindles and rungs tightly to assure a permanent bond. The legs boast of a graceful splay which required delicate balance to achieve and were inserted into holes bored at an angle about three inches in from the chair's bottom. A wedge and glue helped secure the legs which penetrated through to the top of the seat at

Two drawer bedside table, pine and maple. Size: 21″ wide, 19″ deep, 28½″ high.

$145.00 - 165.00

Windsor bow back rocking chair, nine spindles in back. Size: 16½″ to seat, 35″ high.

$175.00 - 200.00

Windsor arm chair, nine spindles at top, H rungs, splayed legs. Size: 17½″ to seat, 38″ high.

$250.00 - 300.00

Windsor bow back chair, bentwood arms, incised lines on legs to position rungs, front stretcher foot worn.

$155.00 - 175.00

times or they could be socketed into holes about three fourths the depth of the seat. The stretchers (rungs) frequently were in an "H"-shaped formation. For beauty, deft colonial craftsmen fashioned pieces not any larger than were necessary to prove functionally sound and combined various woods with differing characteristics to acquire the maximum strength. Steam and molds helped shape and bend the hickory, ash, beech, or birch for the backs while maple, oak, beech, birch, or ash proved satisfactory for turnings. An early Windsor had a thick shield or elliptical-shaped seat formed from one piece of pine or soft birch fashioned to the contour of the human body with symmetrical scoops on either side of a central pommel suggesting a saddle appearance; hence, the term "saddle seat." At times as much as half the bottom might be sculpted away with the aid of an adze, gouging chisel, and block plane. Since there was no apron, the underside would be chamfered (cut in at a slant) to diminish the heavy thick look. Sometimes the chair was left natural, but generally the various woods were united compatibly by paint — the favorite green, with black, red, white, yellow, or brown likewise predominating. Backs varied and carried various descriptive names such as loop-, bow-, fan-, comb-, low-, and arch-back, and some came in petite sizes for tots or were high chairs.

Two exclusively Yankee innovations were the rocking chair and the writing Windsor which has a wide, flat arm supported by spindles set into an extension on the seat and attached more often to the right than to accommodate left-handers. Some say diplomatic statesman author Ben Franklin with his inventive mind put rockers on a straight chair, but others think a rural resident wanted his wife to sit with ease while she nursed the baby and cut off a small section of the legs on a Windsor chair, adding runners from a cradle to form this new combination. There are those who deny the rocker is an American first. They state that archeological digs have uncovered toy versions which emulate people sizes and these precede U.S. examples. Nevertheless, the rocking chair has been adopted from the White House to the prairie and from sea to shining sea.

As time passed, the Windsor changed, gradually declining in charm since the number of spindles diminished, the seat tended to flatten and could be formed of several boards glued together, or might be caned. The rake of the legs was not so pronounced; thus, the graceful proportions and balance tended to be lessened. Many small side chairs with a wide top rail and "sticks" frequently are called rod-back Windsors. The 1700s low-back Windsor was the granddaddy of the "firehouse Windsor" of the mid-1800s, the latter featuring sparsely splayed legs, a

Windsor type Firehouse, captain's, or bar stool, nine spindles, H shape rungs. Size: 17" to seat.

$95.00 - 125.00

slightly saddled seat, and u-shaped arms — a familiar furnishing in fire stations. Riverboat and coastal pilots of the late 1800s liked a debased form which acquired the name "captain's chairs" and lost the saddled, thick seats. These became popular for use in club rooms, country hotels, offices, and courtrooms, and some similar types are referred to as bar stools. They retain their status on factory production lines to this day; thus, it is necessary to check age factors if an old example is sought.

An American chair which aroused European derision in the early 1800s when travelers from abroad tested it was the rocker. As typical as a slab of juicy, spicy apple pie on a restaurant menu, the rocking chair is occasionally feared by non-natives who do not like its creeping motions and fear it will tip over as it tilts backward and forward; yet, many U.S. citizens find this motion restful or therapeutic. When his physician recommended that President John F. Kennedy should sit in a chair with runners to relax his injured back, the chief executive's use of a rocker caused an upswing of interest in this "down home" oriented seat.

The Boston type has been termed by some as the first developed with its own characteristic style and receives its name because it supposedly originated in the city famed for Bunker and Beacon Hills. As does the Windsor, it has a many-spindled back and old examples tend to have more "sticks" (at least seven) with gentle body contour shaping than those of more recent vintage. It appears to be akin to the Hitchcock because of its freehand painted or stenciled rail designs, and salvaging the artwork preserves top price. The thick seat, preferably all in one piece, rolls up in back and curls under at the front.

Lyre-back stencilled rocker, rolled three piece seat, "Stuart-Hale & Co. Makers" in rectangle near bottom of lyre back. Size: 15½" to seat, 20" wide, 14¾" deep.

$155.00 - 175.00

Boston rocker, seven spindles, three piece rolled seat, very narrow runners. Size: 19¾" wide, 16" deep, 40½" high.

$225.00 - 250.00

As the generations passed and new trends developed, the rocking chair resembled a chameleon. Much as this lizard switches colors to blend with its environment, so the rocker through the years has swapped styles to harmonize with changing decorating trends. Some were slouchy and man-sized, some petite, some painted, some sombre. Families tended to give rockers personality by associating them with the person and the purpose for which they were generally occupied. A small version became a sewing rocker if Grandma consistently sat and stitched in her favorite chair, while another family might associate a similar diminutive size with nursing if Mama held her sucking infant as she swayed backward and forward. Large ones where Papa or Grandpa relaxed "of an evening" had their names assigned. A famous name connected with a style is the Lincoln rocker, commonly a black horsehair upholstered chair with a tall contoured back which a long, lean figure would find comfortable. Its arms have a graceful roll.

Rockers span the gap from the sophisticated to the country, with an upholstered, tufted-back, velvet example as stiff and formal as a youth in a rented tuxedo attending his senior prom; to a battered green Boston rocker which might appear as rustic as a hard-working, generation-ago farmer in bib overalls sucking on a corncob pipe. This trait means that the rocking chair proves compatible and companionable in varied settings or in almost any room in the house.

Boston rocker, one piece seat rolls up in back and under in front, black paint with faded yellow floral design.

$200.00 - 225.00

ady's rocker, seven spindles, three piece rolled seat, calloped top slat. Size: 15" to seat, 19" wide, 14" deep.

$155.00 - 185.00

Hitchcock Chairs

"Hitchcock" is the generic term for a style of fancy native side chairs. Similar to a head waiter, Lambert Hitchcock, who began his business around 1820, has seated generations of Americans. It is he who received credit for introducing mass production to the furniture manufacturing industry. Many of his "knocked down" chairs were bought by peddlers whose wagons carted them to rural areas for resale and to be assembled on location since parts were easier to transport than completed units. Bundles of legs and slats stack better than whole chairs do. Midwesterners, northerners, as well as southerners became accustomed to these Hitchcocks with their plank (solid wood), rush, or cane seats, which frequently were artificially grained to resemble imported expensive rosewood or painted with powdered gold accents with the aid of fruit and flower stencils. The top rail in the chair back could be rolled or have a wooden "pillow" feature. At times the middle slat was wide to be decorated generously or was carved to resemble the national emblem, the eagle. Varieties with arms were made much less frequently.

Hitchcock chairs are reminiscent of the fancy styles English furniture designer Thomas Sheraton promoted and which were adapted in this country in the early 1800s. Naturally, when they sold well, the line was emulated by many other factories. All these painted and decorated chairs have come to be lumped under the family title "Hitchcock," but those made at his establishment commonly were stenciled with his name on the back edge of the seat. Those produced from about 1825-29 say "L. Hitchcock, Hitchcocks-ville, Conn. Warranted." When Alford, a relative by marriage, became a partner, the marking switched to "Hitchcock, Alford, & Co., Hitchcocks-ville, Conn. Warranted." and when the partnership dissolved, the circa 1843-52 mark was "Lambert Hitchcock, Unionville, Conn." Antique-wise, it is good to preserve labels which help identify and date a piece. Save the original decoration when possible because most of the surviving chairs from circa 1820 to 1850 have known abuse, their surfaces coated with layers of

Left: Lyre-back fancy chair, basic black with gold fruits and green leaves. Size: 17½" to seat, 15½" wide, 14" deep, 34½" high.

$150.00 - 175.00

Above: Hitchcock-type pillow rail chairs, rush seats, basic black with gold grapes, melons, and leaves. Size: 18" to seat, 17" wide at front to 15" wide at rear, 14½" deep, 34" high.

$200.00 - 250.00 each.

paint which current owners strip off to expose the natural wood; therefore, a purist would be willing to pay an additional fee for examples with the faded stenciling still visible. Chairs of this type are made currently, and it helps to be aware of construction methods and signs of wear to help distinguish the old from the new.

Shaker Furniture

American country furniture was exemplified well by a religious separatist sect, the United Society of Believers, quaintly dubbed Shakers by unbelievers who observed their shaky motions when they danced as a part of their worship ritual. Men with women? Lads with their lassies? Heavens no! They were celibates, and males were in a row on one side quivering and chanting indepently as females lined up in their own ranks. Austerity was a way of life to these immigrants who came from England under the leadership of Sister Ann Lee (originally Lees) in 1774 to establish their own communities. Since members were forbidden to marry, the only children were those in the families of already married converts or those the group adopted. This lack of procreation caused the Believers to fade gradually in vitality and numbers, but during their height, they were powerful. Their belief that work was worship caused them to toil hard for the glory of God as they sought perfection in all their tasks which were assigned according to their aptitudes. The Shakers are credited with developing and inventing labor-saving devices including washing machines, cheese presses, better brooms, farm implements and machinery, and improved seeds. Their buildings, in which "the sisters" and "the brothers" had their separate entrances, stairways, and quarters, were beautiful in the simplicity of their design, and their unique furniture was likewise plain, staunch, sturdy, utilitarian. When the U.S. Government selected native workmanship to be displayed in a World Exposition in Japan in the early 1970s, Shaker furnishings with their uncluttered lines were conspicuously in view. The colonies, located in various states such as New York, Maine, Massachusetts, Connecticut, Ohio, and Kentucky, sold Shaker products including quality garden seeds, brooms, and furniture to non-members. What could be handier and more

Shaker-type rush seat rocker, carpet cutter runners.
$150.00 - 175.00

91

homey than a slat back sewing rocker with a built-in drawer placed under the woven seat where material, needles, thread, and scissors could be always available? Shaker unadorned, well proportioned furnishings were fashioned from indigenous woods — pine, maple, walnut, or fruitwoods. There are collectors who seek Shaker articles, and some do turn up at shops or sales, but it is easiest to see these works at museums. The sect began selling chairs as the 1700s waned, and, in the 1850s, had standard numbers on their products. They also identified them by applying a gold transfer trademark with the Shaker name included. Magazines frequently publish patterns so that copies of their uncluttered craft efforts can be made by home handymen.

The Society sold attractive slat-back chairs in various styles which appeared fragile but were actually sturdy. Others produced similar types, but the Shaker versions are especially appreciated for their gracefulness. When a chair has a series of slats (run horizontally) as back supports, it reminds one of ladder rungs with the cross pieces ascending from the seat, and the popular name applied is "ladder-back" chair. Various materials from nature were woven to form seats. Splint, thin, flat strips of hickory or oak, may appear in various patterns such as a series of triangles slanting across or in a straight block design, but a molded paper imitation splint is available currently. Twisted and rolled paper is usually used today to rush seats with their four equal adjoining triangles. It replaces the marsh-grown flag formerly employed. Cane made from rattan (climbing palm with slender, long, tough stems) commonly forms a pattern which resembles rows of diamonds, but a clever caner produces other designs as well. A synthetic material is available, but many antiquers prefer the natural cane. Some chairs have a woven seat and back both. The Shakers found that various colors of fabric tape could be combined to create attractive patterns. Designated "brothers" made the frames, and assigned "sisters" completed the weaving steps on the bottoms. If slats were not used to form the backs, they could be woven and were cheerful when done with the bright tapes.

The listed groupings represent the primary categories of country seats and tables.

Stool, rush seat, H turned stretchers, splayed legs. Size: 24" wide, 10" deep, 21" high.

$65.00 - 90.00

Footstool, walnut and pine. Size: Top – 10" x 7", 10" high.

$40.00 - 45.00

Stool, splayed legs with feet turned at base. Size: 11¾" diameter, 23" high.

$45.00 - 65.00

Stool, pine, three splayed legs. Size: 9½" diameter, 19" high.

$35.00 - 55.00

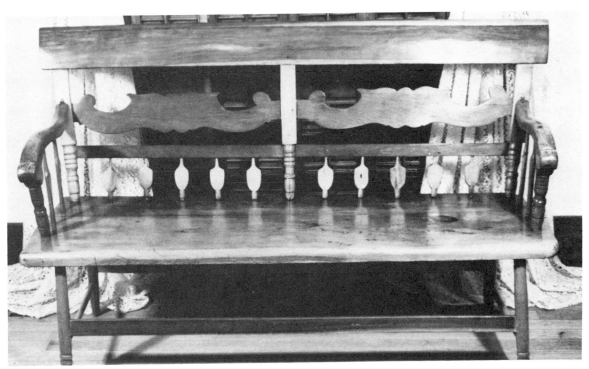

Arrowback settee. Size: 53½" wide, 17" deep, 16¼" to seat, 35" high.

$1,000.00 - 1,100.00

Windsor settee or deacon's bench, pine. Size: 71½" wide, 14½" deep, 31½" high.
$575.00 - 625.00

Above: Deacon's bench, maple and poplar. Size: 75½" wide, 19½" deep.
$575.00 - 625.00

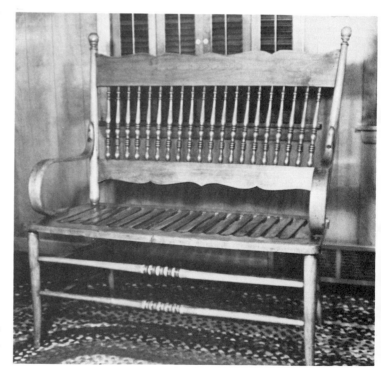

Slat seat bench, maple and hickory. Size: 40" wide, 18" deep, 17¾" to seat, 41" high.
$350.00 - 400.00

Drop leaf table, maple and walnut. Size: 39″ wide, 19″ deep, 28″ high, 14½″ drop leaves.

$225.00 - 250.00

Drop leaf table, maple. Size: 42″ wide, 17½″ deep, 29½″ high, 11¼″ drop leaves.

$200.00 - 225.00

Farm table, pine, legs pegged to apron. Size: 72″ wide, 35½″ deep, 31¼″ high.
$350.00 - 400.00

Country dining table, pine, button turned legs, breadboard ends on top. Size: 63¾″ wide, 38¼″ deep, 30″ high.
$325.00 - 375.00

Above: Hutch or settle table with top down.

Right: Hutch or settle table, pine, drawer in seat, four pins to hold top down. Size: Base – 32″ wide, 16½″ deep, 59″ diameter.

$700.00 - 750.00

Tavern-type table, oak, four box-like receptacles beneath top held beverages, early 1900s. Size: 42″ wide, 31″ deep, 30″ high.
$275.00 - 325.00

Stretcher table, poplar, pine, cherry, walnut, and maple. Size: 32″ wide, 23½″ deep, 24″ high.

$225.00 - 250.00

Tavern table, pine. Size: 24″ wide, 24″ deep, 30″ high.

$125.00 - 150.00

Round top extension table, cherry. Size: 42″ diameter, 27″ high.

$400.00 - 450.00

Drop leaf table, cherry, maple, and pine, one drawer, three to four inches added to bottom of legs to repair water damage. Size: 35″ wide, 18½″ deep, 30″ high.

$250.00 - 275.00

Bedside table, poplar and pine. 19″ wide, 19″ deep, 29½″ high.

$145.00 - 165.00

Country table, Hepplewhite influence. Size: 26½″ wide, 21¼″ deep, 27″ high.

$135.00 - 155.00

Above: Bedside table, cherry and maple, each leg is turned differently, hand pegged construction. Size: 20″ wide, 18½″ deep, 28¾″ high.

$185.00 - 215.00

Right: Dressing table, pine, spool turned legs and stretcher, drop finials at corners. Size: 30″ wide, 16″ deep, 28″ high.

$135.00 - 155.00

Above: Bedside table, cherry. Size: 20″ wide, 17½″ deep, 30″ high.

$150.00 - 175.00

Left: Nightstand, one drawer, walnut and cherry, pegged construction (see legs). Size: 25″ wide, 24″ deep, 30½″ high.

$215.00 - 245.00

Above: Dressing table, walnut, scalloped edge on top. Size: 29″ wide, 19½″ deep, 28½″ high.

$155.00 - 175.00

Right: Drop leaf sewing stand, cherry. Size: 21½″ wide, 15½″ deep, 28½″ high.

$300.00 - 350.00

Armchair, Sheraton influence, rush seat, arrow back. Size: 16½" to seat, 19¼" wide, 33" high.
$325.00 - 350.00

Rush seat, ladder back chair, oak. Size: 18" to seat, 18½" wide, 42" high.
$70.00 - 80.00

Rush seat chair, maple. Size: 17½" to seat, 18½" wide, 34" high.
$65.00 - 75.00

Rush seat, ladder back chair, maple and oak. Size: 16½" to seat, 18½" wide, 15½" deep, 36" high.
$65.00 - 80.00

Splint seat, ladder back chair, maple. Size: 14"
to seat.

$60.00 - 70.00

Splint seat, ladder back chair. Size: 13½" to
seat.

$55.00 - 65.00

Fireside chair, splint seat, ladder back. Size:
12" to seat.

$55.00 - 65.00

Splint seat, ladder back chair. Size: 15" to
seat.

$65.00 - 80.00

Rush seat chair, slat back. Size: 18″ to seat, 16½″ wide, 13½″ deep, 33″ high.
$95.00 - 110.00

Tape woven chair, splat back. Size: 16″ to seat, 16½″ wide, 15½″ deep, 37½″ high.
$95.00 - 110.00

Hitchcock-type pillow rail arm chair, basic black with gold grapes, melons, and leaves. Size: 18″ to seat, 18″ wide at front to 15½″ wide at rear, 15½″ deep, 34″ high.
$300.00 - 350.00

Pennsylvania Dutch fancy chair, plank seat, yellow, blue design on splat. Size: 15″ wide, 13″ deep, 31″ high.
$150.00 - 175.00

Rod-back armchair. Size: 17¼" to seat, 18" wide, 16" deep, 32½" high.

$145.00 - 165.00

Rod-back armchair, cherry, basswood (seat), maple, and poplar, 1¾" plank seat. Size: 15½" to seat, 18½" wide, 15½" deep, 32½" high.

$135.00 - 155.00

Rod-back armchair, maple and basswood. Size: 17" to seat, 19" wide, 14" deep, 33" high.

$125.00 - 145.00

One-half spindle plank seat chair. $55.00 - 65.00

One-half spindle plank seat chair.
$75.00 - 90.00

One-half spindle plank seat chair.
$55.00 - 65.00

One-half spindle plank seat chair.
$55.00 - 65.00

One-half spindle plank seat chair. Size: 16" to
seat, 15½" wide, 32" high.
$110.00 - 125.00

One-half spindle plank seat chair, pine, ash, maple.

$75.00 - 90.00

Rod-back Windsor. Size: 17" to seat.
$60.00 - 70.00

One-half spindle plank seat chair, maple and ash.

$75.00 - 90.00

Rod-back Windsor. Size: 17" to seat.
$60.00 - 70.00

Rod-back Windsor. Size: 16¾" to seat.
$60.00 - 70.00

Plank seat chair, bamboo turnings, mixed
light woods. Size: 15½" wide, 14½" deep,
33" high.
$65.00 - 75.00

Hoop-back, plank seat chair. Size: 17" to seat,
17" wide, 32" high.
$45.00 - 65.00

Windsor chair, Sheraton influence, "C.
Sheppard" in capitals impressed in bottom of
seat, legs go through seat. Size: 17½" to
seat, 34" high.
$175.00 - 195.00

Windsor chair, continuous arm from seat around back and to seat in one piece. Size: 15″ to seat, 29½″ high.

$95.00 - 110.00

Windsor, firehouse, captain's chair, or bar stool. Size: 17″ to seat, 19″ wide, 20″ deep, 32″ high.

$125.00 - 145.00

Windsor comb-back chair, one piece forms arms and back. Size: 17¼″ to seat, 17½″ wide, 18″ deep, 32″ high.

$95.00 - 125.00

Windsor chair, continuous arm. Size: 22¼″ wide, 18″ deep, 30″ high.

$125.00 - 145.00

Windsor chair, bar type, H stretcher. Size: 17" to seat, 1¾" thick seat.
$95.00 - 110.00

Windsor chair, bar type, hickory, ash, and maple. Size: 17¼" to seat.
$95.00 - 100.00

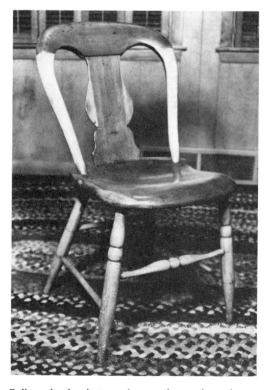

Balloon-back chair, ash, maple, and poplar. Size: 17" to seat, 16" wide, 31" high.
$125.00 - 145.00

Pressed-back rocker. Size: 12½" wide, 12½" deep, 30" high.
$130.00 - 145.00

Woven herringbone pattern rocker, bamboo type turnings.

$95.00 - 115.00

Woven splint seat rocking chair, maple. Size: 13" to seat, 33" high.

$85.00 - 100.00

Shaker-type rocking chair, woven seat, maple.

$175.00 - 200.00

One-half arm, rush seat rocking chair, late eighteenth century. Size: 17" to seat, 41" high.

$295.00 - 325.00

Chapter 6
The Bedchamber

The bedchamber of yesteryear sponsored family members from the cradle to the grave. Babies were born at home and ya-yahed their first spank-induced cries in the parental bed where they were conceived. Death, too, hovered in the home in days when hospitalization was unavailable or certainly uncommon. Since a human slumbers about one third of life away, sleeping accommodations are important.

A supporting frame around a sacking filled with some soft stuffing was commonly made of wood but metal (iron or brass) could be utilized. This was a bedstead, but through the years the terminology has changed so that the "stead" has been dropped and "bed" has remained to designate a place to sleep.

Rope Beds

An example which retained its popularity from about the 1820s through the 1880s was the rope bedstead. Instead of metal springs over slats to uphold the filled ticking, ropes were strung in parallel lines from pegs spaced equidistant on the wooden rails. The lacings went around the pegs from head to foot as well as crossing from side to side. This webbing sagged after repeated usage, and part of the housekeeping tasks included keeping it taut. A small wooden two-pronged instrument which sometimes resembled an enlarged wooden clothespin was frequently employed to twist the ropes tight. When the bedposts terminated with a ball finial, the name "cannonball bed" described this feature. Carved pineapples were also utilized.

Jenny Lind Spool Beds

In addition to this heavy style, many early spool beds have laced systems since slats to support mattresses did not become prominent until about the time of the Civil War (circa 1861). Spool beds can be bourgeoisie or elite depending on their construction, wood, or the appointments which accompany them. They received their name because the turnings resemble a series of spools strung together with variations which include button lookalikes and elongated spool forms. The famous United States circus showman P.T. Barnum imported and promoted the adored opera singer, Jenny Lind, billed as the "Swedish Nightingale." Her singing delighted audiences and her concerts were sold out in the cities where she appeared in 1850-52. Miss Lind donated to philanthropic causes such as funding a frontier chapel in a midwestern Swedish-oriented community where the lumber the residents accumulated to build a church became coffins instead when a cholera epidemic beleaguered the population. She provided financial aid to a free Negro mother who eagerly sought a similar status for her enslaved offsprings. The knowledge of Jenny's generosity increased her popularity until men, dressed in their best suits to attend her concert, loosened her horses and placed themselves "in harness" to pull her carriage triumphantly through the streets in Cincinnati, Ohio. Because of her wide appeal, products were named for Jenny Lind just as today there are games endorsed by television personalities or T-shirts emblazoned with a star's figure. In the 1850s, there were dolls made to resemble the singer, and spool furniture took on her name, especially spool beds. Those with square corners are older than rounded versions because it was easier to make straight turnings on a lathe than curved ones. Early frames were mainly of maple but walnut and cherry also appeared. Soft woods, including pine, were usual after 1850. Spool furniture was popular from 1820-1870 and is still made.

Purchasers of antique beds should be wary because people in earlier generations (with exceptions such as Presidents Washington, Jefferson, Monroe, and Lincoln) tended to be short in stature, and today's taller people require six foot plus beds. This means that rails must be replaced or enlarged lengthwise to accommodate modern mattress sizes. Double beds and single beds were sold, but at times, width measurements were about three-quarters of the present standard norm. If the bed is used as is, a custom made mattress may be required, so do consider necessary adjustments and comfort when purchasing old bed frames.

A visit to West Branch, Iowa, to the humble, Quaker home of Herbert Hoover, the first United States president born west of the Mississippi River (natal year, 1874), shows how space can be utilized well. With two tiny rooms to house five people during a snowy, blowy Iowa winter, Papa and Mama slept in a bedstead. Herbert and his brother huddled together in a low trundle rolled out at night from its daily storage space beneath the adult bed while baby sister swayed gently in a cradle.

Rope bed, maple. Size: 52" wide, 75" long.
$350.00 - 400.00

Jenny Lind spool bed. Size: 50" wide, 76" long.
$375.00 - 400.00

Cradle, pine. Size: 43" long, 20" wide, 14¾" high at wings.
$225.00 - 250.00

Painted Furniture including Cottage Suites

Some low-cost furnishings were artificially grained to resemble a rarer or more expensive wood. A poplar chest could be painted a reddish-brown hue, gently ribbon streaked with black, and a modest home had a "mahogany" dresser. Fancy imported rosewood was faked freely. An 1880s ad lists artificial walnut at a lower price than the grained simulated imported woods commanded. While a three piece imitation walnut bedroom suite retailed for $23 to $30, a similar mahogany set cost three dollars more. Feathers, combs, brushes, sponges, or the like provided lines which were stroked on with care to provide varied effects.

Years ago, if a fellow loved a girl and wanted to tell her so, he might make a chest with a lift lid (trunk like) especially for her so she could fill it with homemade sheets, quilts, towels, and other linens in anticipation of the day they would wed. At times a papa made his little girl a dowry or hope chest where she could tuck away linens until she grew up and married and took her dowry to her new home with her.

Some of these colorful gifts were "Pennsylvania Dutch" in origin. Upon their arrival in the seventeenth and eighteenth centuries, European immigrants from the Rhineland said they were "Deutsch" which means "German," but their new neighbors misunderstood and, misinterpreting, called these people the "Pennsylvania Dutch" even though they were not natives of Holland. They painted chests with neat panels containing flowers, birds, hearts, or angels. Many were made from the early 1700s through the middle of the nineteenth century. Immigrants from the Scandinavian countries likewise delighted in a vivid flare of colors and executed all-over designs, not limiting their display to specified panels as the "Deutsch" did. True collectors preserve the faded tones of yesteryear as folk art gems.

Cottage suites were a delight. A bed, chest of drawers, washstand, and table made from an inexpensive wood or a mixture of species could be painted so that all matched. After the surface dried, it would be decorated, generally with bright stencil designs of fruits, flowers, or birds. Apple blossoms and geraniums could radiate beauty all year round. In 1836, "Deacon" William Haldane used hand tools in his home to construct the first commercial furniture available to frontiersmen in and around Grand Rapids, Michigan, the city which later was to be designated "the furniture capital" of the United States. Many factories were established there since lumber from the nearby forests was abundant and easy to secure. In the winter, bobsleds, gliding across the snow, could transport a year's

Blanket chest, bracket feet, artificially grained. Size: 42½" wide, 16¾" deep, 19¾" high.

$150.00 - 175.00

112

Dowry chest, brass bail handles, dovetailed corners, poplar wood. Size: 41" wide, 19" deep, 20" high.
$200.00 - 225.00

Four piece cottage bedroom suite, soft blue panels with flowers and leaves and crane on head and footboard. "J. H. Crane's Furniture Warerooms S. E. corner of 4th St. and Washington Ave., St Louis, Mo.," stamped on back of bedstead.

$1,500.00 - 1,750.00

supply of wood for the local mills. The city's New England Furniture Company promoted softwood enameled bedroom suites that could be ornamented to coordinate with or match drapery fabrics, carpets, or wallpapers. A set which included an elaborate bed, a towel rack, three chairs, a dressing case, and a commode was priced at $25 in 1880. Across the country, in Boston, the firm of Meriam & Parsons advertised cottage chamber (bedroom) furniture in the 1860s and 70s. Bureaus, wardrobes, sinks, tables, toilets, washstands, and chairs could be secured there. Various New York firms sold fancy chairs and ornamental furniture to augment the color trend and to supply ordinary families with low-cost, attractive suites.

For a multitude of years, the undiscerning have stripped the mellowed outer layers off, immune to their soft folk-type decor, and have sought the pine, poplar, or other natural woods beneath. A purist would beg that designs, even though incomplete, should be retained although the paint is worn off in spots. Heritage folk art flows away when the remover and sander take over.

A bedroom is expected to have accommodations for the apparel of its occupants. Clothes were commonly hung on hooks fastened to the wall or placed in freestanding closets. If one chooses to be fancy, such wardrobes could be called "armoires" because centuries previously such cupboards were storage units for arms and armor. Since these closets can be huge and heavy, many have removable pegs which enable the sides, top, bottom, shelves, and back to come apart. Collapsed in this manner, the pieces can be transported easily, carried up and down stairs, around corners, and through narrow doorways — an impossible chore when they are fully assembled, cumbersome, wide, tall heavyweights.

Chests, dressers, and bureaus with simple lines have a rustic appearance. Although many are constructed from woods with light tones, dark hardwoods can be unadorned and primitively executed. Trunks or boxes store articles well, and a father might design such a container for a designated purpose; for example, the precisely correct length to hold the long skirts his daughter wore at the turn of this century so they would not develop creases from being folded. After all, every fashionable female wore blouses and ankle-covering skirts during that time period. If someone owned seasonal garmets (dark woolens for winter, lighter fabrics for summer), they could be tucked away in attic trunks when they were not needed.

The extent of the bedchamber furniture helped reflect the financial status of the family. Pioneers who pushed through the wilderness, thrifty people, and the indigent did not demand extensive suites. Of course, before water was piped into houses, a wash bowl was standard equipment in the kitchen, and a winter bathing area near the cooking heat source was available by carrying in a tub to fill with water; but bedrooms also had their bowls and pitchers. Washstands and commodes held utilitarian "toilet" supplies and the emergency potty peeked modestly from beneath the bed. Water accommodating furnishings are discussed in Chapter 3, "The Plumbing Problem."

An item which could be included in a bedroom is the desk, which evolved from a box, although usually it would occupy a more prominent position in a more frequented area. If a frontier home owned a book, it was generally the Bible which could be placed in its own box, minus any locking device. After all, who would be wicked enough to steal God's word as contained in the Good Book? Those who were fortunate enough to know how to read and write might record family marriages, births, and deaths within its covers.

A portable box to hold writing materials and important papers or documents would have a lock. Gradually a slant lift lid was utilized and when it was placed

Counter desk, pine. Size: 20½" wide, 17" deep, 7½" high at front, 12" high at back.

$95.00- 110.00

Wardrobe, assembled with pegs so can be disassembled. Size: 46" wide, 18½" deep, 77½" high.

$400.00 - 450.00

kirt box, made specifically to hold skirts. Size: 46" wide, 20½" deep, 19¾" high. $135.00 - 155.00

on a leg frame, a writer could sit at a desk. Later improvements included drawers in the base, a drop lid with the hinges at the front instead of the rear so that the surface did not have to be cleared when some article stored inside was sought, and book shelves above, which provided additional space. These switches and changes commenced in the late 1600s and early 1700s as desks became more utilitarian, and many varieties were spawned, but this book spurns the elegant to concentrate on the casual.

These pieces comprised bedroom furnishings, but actually, a bedstead required only a corner of a one-room cabin, a space in a loft, or it could be the main article in a "chamber." The simple versions spell "country."

Single bed, poplar, maple, ash, and oak. Size: 79" long, 44" wide, 56" high at headboard.
$325.00 - 350.00

Bureau washstand, pine, used in a hotel, panel ends. Size: 37" wide, 16" deep, 34" high.
$195.00 - 225.00

Bureau washstand, cherry. Size: 37" wide, 18½" deep, 30¾" high.

$265.00 - 285.00

Bureau washstand, pine, escutcheons for decoration only. Size: 30¼" wide, 14½" deep, 35" high.

$175.00 - 200.00

Blanket chest, pine. Size: 39" wide, 28" deep, 34" high.

$200.00 - 225.00

Blanket box, pine, lift top. Size: 38" wide, 20" deep, 36" high.

$450.00 - 500.00

Modified corner cupboard, pine, wainscot doors. Size: 46″ wide, 12″ deep, 68″ high.
$200.00 - 225.00

Wardrobe, poplar. Size: 35¾″ wide, 17¾″ deep, 65½″ high.
$195.00 - 235.00

Table top desk, pine, maple, butternut. Size: 42″ wide, 29″ deep, 29″ high.
$275.00 - 300.00

Towel rack, pine. Size: 34″ high.
$65.00 - 75.00

Desk, walnut, pegged doors, pigeon holes in each half. Size: 33" wide, 11½" deep, 32" high.

$400.00 - 425.00

Lady's desk, cherry, top of base is hinged and lifts up and back. Size: 32" wide, 22" deep, 68" high.

$950.00 - 1,050.00

Lift top desk, maple. Size: 37" wide, 24" deep, 28" high.

$375.00 - 400.00

Cupboard top, fall front desk, walnut. Size: 34" wide, 20" deep at base, 74" high.

$650.00 - 750.00

Secretary desk, butternut, two pieces, drop front exposes compartments. Size: 41½" wide, 21½" deep at base, 90¼" high.
$1,200.00 - 1,300.00

Two piece drop lid desk with bookcase top, pine. Size: 48" wide, 24" deep, 78" high.
$1,200.00 - 1,300.00

Trunk, hide covered. Size: 24" wide, 14" deep, 11" high.
$85.00 - 100.00

Trunk, pine, rounded top, dovetailed corners. Size: 38½" wide, 17" deep, 16½" high.
$145.00 - 165.00

Institutional desk, plantation type, ash, artificially grained. Size: 39″ wide, 30″ deep, 62″ high.
$950.00 - 1,000.00

Rose cap, corner combination cupboard and desk, pine. Size: 30″ deep to corner, 87¼″ high.
$575.00 - 650.00

runk, walnut, dovetailed corners. Size: 35½″ wide, 21″ ep, 17¾″ high.
$165.00 - 185.00

Trunk, banded with wrought iron straps attached with brass headed tacks. Size: 29″ wide, 16″ deep, 16″ high.
$110.00 - 125.00

Trunk, pine, large dovetailed corners, bail handles. Size: 29½" wide, 11" deep, 12½" high.
$145.00 - 165.00

Trunk, pine, dovetailed corners, metal corner pieces at base. Size: 36" wide, 21" deep, 26" high.
$160.00 - 175.00

Trunk, pine, dovetailed corners, bracket base. Size: 36" wide, 19" deep, 22" high.
$145.00 - 165.00

Trunk, bail handles, dated 1867, dovetailed corners.

$200.00 - 250.00

Sugar chest, pine with walnut pegged legs. Size: 45" wide, 20" deep, 27" high.

$385.00 - 400.00

Utility box, pine. Size: 12½" wide, 9½" deep, 7½" high.

$55.00 - 65.00

Chest, flat top, molding above legs, pine, one board sides, front, and top. Size: 43" wide, 17½" deep, 22" high.

$175.00 - 200.00

Trunk, pine, rounded top, dated 1795. Size: 39" wide, 25" deep, 24" high.

$375.00 - 400.00

Trunk, pine, metal bands, bail handles. Size: 30" wide, 15½" deep, 20" high.

$145.00 - 165.00

Trunk, pine, leather handles, ornate brass escutcheon. 29" wide, 16" deep, 18¼" high.

$150.00 - 175.00

Utility box, pine. Size: 34½″ wide, 12″ deep, 16″ high.

$95.00 - 125.00

Bride's box, pine, handle on top, large key. Size: 20″ wide, 13″ deep, 10½″ high.

$125.00 - 150.00

Trunk, pine. Size: 29″ wide, 15″ deep, 15″ high.

$125.00 - 145.00

Chapter 7
'Bye Baby Bunting

A friend exuding pride remarked, "For years I watched antique highchairs leap pricewise by ten, fifteen dollars annually until finally I decided if I wanted to own one, I'd better buy it for the grandchild I anticipated having someday. I acquired the chair first, and now, *I have the grandchild!*"

In reality, a baby doesn't require an abundance of accessories. A built-in loud bawl commands attention and lets one know immediately when something is amiss. A place to sleep, accommodations for eating, a dry clean bottom, and provisions for lots of cuddling and loving are basics to keep infantile feet kicking and arms waving contentedly. However, adults who coo and chant over the "tiny bundles from heaven" enjoy providing them with many extras. Traditionally, while the females knitted or sewed to prepare necessary garments, proud papas-to-be and granddads worked with wood to turn out beds, cradles, toys, highchairs, or other small furnishings for the little ones. Cabinet makers catered to the public by producing such objects, and when the factory system was inaugurated, companies capitalized on the parental desire to provide well for their progeny.

Tiny tots' belongings delight many, both because they can be functional and because miniature sizes seem to fit almost anywhere and are fun to own. There isn't much that comprises adult furnishings which has not been scaled down for the "young uns." The slat or ladder back straight chair and rocker come in youthful sizes. Emulating the adults', one could have woven seats of rush, cane, splint, or tape, and weaving could form the back as well as the bottom.

Child's ladder back chair, rush seat. Size: 7" to seat, 23" high.
$200.00 - 225.00

Also in chair styles, consider the Windsor with its "stick" construction, many of them late versions with fewer of these spindles, less splay (slant) to the legs, and solid plank seats which are not body contoured as early examples were. For little people there are straight chairs, rockers, highchairs, and swaying cradles where the spindle look prevails. Many Sunday Schools in the early 1900s had bow-back Windsors for their beginner and primary classes which oldsters can recall sitting in as they sang, listened to stories, or repeated verses. With genuine effort, a child could lift and carry a chair from the story area to a long, low table where a student could color a picture to take home. Occasionally one sees a school table in a home duplicating as a coffee table.

The Boston rocker, popular with adults, occurs in petite versions. As in its grown-up counterpart, the small sizes were customarily fashioned from a variety of woods and painted a solid color such as black or green to be decorated over with gold scrolls, fruits, or flowers. Their continuous popularity keeps them in furniture production lines today. Check chapter two to see how to detect the old from the new.

Naturally, tables come in diminutive sizes and varying styles, and some fold up so that they can be put away in a small space if desired. Desks were made with youngsters in mind, and one early form is a lift lid set on legs. It is not unusual to find schoolroom discards serving children in their homes or being used as little hall or porch pieces. A classroom desk can be a single unit, which includes a seat or the bench, may not be connected, and can function separately. A friend enjoys writing worthy or cheerful mottoes on an old-time slate for her family's edification. One such as Ben Franklin's admonition, "Early to bed, early to rise, makes a man healthy, wealthy, and wise," makes a fitting introduction to the next paragraph.

Above: Child's Boston rocker, three piece seat. Size: 11" to seat, 13¼" wide, 14" deep, 24¼" high.
$125.00 - 145.00
Left: Windsor highchair, foot rest has been added. Size: 31" high. $110.00 - 135.00

Beds of dainty stature with a rustic feel could have the strung rope supports for mattresses. Spool turnings may be "country-ish," and beds or cradles of this type accommodated children. In some families it is traditional to pass a cradle down from generation to generation. Family heritage receives stress when someone says to a youngster, "Your grandpa and your great aunts were rocked in that cradle. When your mommie was a baby, she slept in it; and when you were born, it was your turn. Some day when you grow up and get married, you may rock your child in it."

Generally cradles sway from side to side, but there are some who maintain it is more natural to have a backward and forward motion such as is experienced when one sits in a rocking chair. Because of this, they put the runners on lengthwise instead of across the width, and there are those who insist that this helps deter colic. There are suspended cradles which hang from frames and platform types.

Child's lift top desk, maple and ash. Size: 29" wide, 20" deep, 28½" high.
$150.00 - 175.00

Cradle, pine and poplar, hand holds on sides, wings to stop draft. Size: 35" long, 14½" wide, 14" high.
$155.00 - 185.00

Hooded cradle, pine. Size: 34" long, 12" wide, 24½" high.
$275.00 - 300.00

At one time, people believed that night air promoted lung disorders, and cradles were made with solid sides and hoods to ward off drafts. Baby was well protected in this hide-away which was frequently formed from easy-to-work pine or poplar wood. Some examples date back to the 1600s, but naturally, those made in the 1800s are more prevalent.

Small girls who wanted to play at being mother might own delicate trunks to keep favorite possessions in. Even dolly could have a dainty place for her own clothing, and the trunk could be made of very thin wood, often with a grained paper covering, since it was not constructed to hold hefty articles.

Proud papas (and doting grandpas too) frequently made "play toys" for their offspring, which now serve as ornaments, planters, coffee tables, magazine holders, fireplace wood containers, or as hobby display centers. For example, when a sheet of glass is placed over the bed of a wagon, it can duplicate in many of these capacities. Another ride-upon that provided pleasure was a wooden scooter. "Dashing through the snow" could be quite spectacular in a gaily colored sleigh, and the painted designs from a past generation are worthy of preservation, enhancing the value of the article.

Some people refer to replicas of adult possessions fashioned in tiny sizes as "salesmen's samples." Articles were carried about the countryside to show prospective buyers what wares were available, the quality of the workmanship, finishes, and hardware, the wood utilized, construction details, or how items functioned. It was not until photography was well developed that catalogs provided

Child's trunk, pine, dovetailed corners. Size: 12" wide, 7" deep, 5½" high.
$65.00 - 75.00

Child's painted sleigh. Size: 52½" long, 15¼" wide.
$500.00 - 550.00

instant advertising. Grand Rapids, Michigan, history spinners say that prior to 1862 traveling salesmen had full scale samples or small models of the products they promoted. In 1837, steamships plied the rivers, and land travel was considered an uncertain hardship. By 1855, a plank road permitted horse-drawn vehicles to transport goods and passengers; and railroads reached this frontier area in 1858. After that, it was common practice for an established furniture company to charter a railroad car, and a salesman or the manufacturer himself would move from town to town to peddle wares or take orders from his track headquarters. In 1862, when Elias Matter decided to have photographs made of furniture and printed in book form called a catalogue, models were no longer required. While these statements attest to the existence of small scale replicas, it is a mistake to dub all petite size furnishings "salesmen's samples" since children then, as now, enjoyed playing with objects resembling those their parents owned.

Adults today pounce upon these childhood treasures of yore and the pint-sized populous frequently does not get to enjoy them any more. Perhaps because of nostalgia, they are quickly claimed by the oldsters, some of whom recall their youths through them; or if it is an inherited object, they may proudly proclaim, "This belonged to my grandma." Doll collectors snatch up many to display their unreal "children" in natural settings, and plenty of men seek mechanical toys, trains, or banks from bygone eras. Currently, collecting play things and youthful objects from the past is not a part of a child's world. Grown up "kids" like them too much.

Child's dresser, pine. Size: 16" wide, 8" deep, 12" high.

$85.00 - 100.00

Child's doll cradle, pine. Size: 26"
long, 14½" wide, 17½" high.
$75.00 - 95.00

Wooden scooter, oak.
$90.00 - 110.00

Wooden wagon, oak. Size: 31½"
long, 14" wide.
$125.00 - 145.00

Rod-back Windsor highchair. Size: 22½″ to seat, 34″ high.

$125.00 - 145.00

Windsor highchair. Size: 22″ to seat, 12″ wide, 11″ deep, 29¾″ high.

$75.00 - 95.00

Above: Child's table, pine. Size: 24″ wide, 16½″ deep, 18″ high.

$110.00 - 135.00

Left: Windsor rocking chair, comb back. Size: 9″ to seat, 18½″ high.

$85.00 - 100.00

Woven cane seat and back child's rocking chair. Size: 10″ to seat, 25″ high.

$95.00 - 110.00

Child's splint seat chair. Size: 13½″ to seat, 27½″ high.

$45.00 - 55.00

Child's table, walnut and pine. Size: 22″ wide, 15½″ deep, 18¾″ high.

$95.00 - 110.00

Toy coffee grinder. Size: 3″ wide, 2½″ deep, 3½″ high.

$40.00 - 50.00

Chapter 8
Primarily Primitive

What do people collect? Practically anything.

How about this? Funeral articles appeal to certain individuals, but others shiver and shun them. A young woman asked a dealer for a coffin table, and the storekeeper gasped, "What's that?" The shopper replied that years ago a family member was "laid out" at home instead of at a mortuary, and the casket was placed on a platform provided for this purpose. It was such a long low table that the young woman sought. Small size coffins, brass or silver plates from caskets, and a substantial wicker oval basket with straps and clasps used to transport a body from the hospital to the undertaking establishment are some of the objects that have been seen with sale tags on them in antique shops.

Two women were overheard conversing. One remarked, "I wish my mother could have enjoyed the modern conveniences I have. She never owned a dishwasher or an automatic washing machine and dryer. She had an ice box in which to keep food cold, and, as the ice melted, she had to empty the drip pan underneath or the water would overflow, spilling all over the place."

The other woman, a retired farmer's wife, nodded assent. Perhaps pictures of her daily duties in previous years were kaleidoscoping before her eyes. For instance, meal preparation took time. No instant mixes or frozen convenience foods were available in her young married days. If she wanted to serve chicken, she had to catch several squawking three or four pounders in the flock, chop their heads off, plunge them into boiling hot water in order to loosen and pluck the feathers. She singed off the hair, cut them up, discarding undesirable portions, washed, and fried them crispy in golden melted butter. If she wanted sweet corn, beans, or tomatoes, she picked them and fixed them for the table. Fruit for pies and sauces required preparation. All the dishes, pots, and silverware had to be washed afterwards in a pan full of sudsy, stove-heated hot water, rinsed, and towel dried. That was merely one mealtime assignment.

Chopping block, maple, used originally for chickens. Size: 28" diameter, 22" high.

$145.00 - 165.00

Just perhaps, a similar picture appeared in her mind before she answered, "I wish I'd had some of today's labor saving devices when my kids were small so I could have spent more time enjoying them."

Despite the comments, generations past were not aware of anything missing. That was life as they knew it. It's strange that today's homemakers hunt out discarded chopping blocks, old washers, wringers, and other inconvenient articles which were associated with hard work. They serve in new decorative or utilitarian capacities in modern homes. Occasionally, a young person zooms back in years to make butter in a churn or accepts a wood burning stove to cut down heating costs, but mainly such time-was articles are not expected to fulfill their former fuctions today.

Before milking machines, the farmer knew his cows by name and was aware of their various personalities. Mollie was placid, always gentle. Bess was stubborn, hard to milk, and would kick over a pail any time she could. The little stool the farmer sat on as he milked could be a flat piece of log with three legs poked through holes in the round seat. Many such hand-fashioned refugees from barns are available and are exposed in homes. Incubators are accepted as casual tables. Animal or human yokes may serve as signs or form wall decorations from which macrame hangings dangle. Outside, a wagon wheel may become a trellis to which red roses cling, or inside, it may be attached to a ceiling to hold lights. Lanterns, electrified or as is, have received a reprieve. Buggy and wagon seats are still places to sit, form coffee tables, or are book depositories. Old grain measures function as waste baskets, toy containers, or serve whatever purpose the imagination demands. Milk cans become stools, umbrella stands, or painted urns. Horse bits frame tiny pictures or contain towels, and horse collars frame mirrors or are converted into clever hanging whatnot shelves. Grain bins which once held wheat and oats to supplement the hay for animals are refinished for indoors so one could truthfully say that barnyard items are considered "in" among those who enjoy primitives.

Milking stool, oak and maple. Size: 10½" diameter, 11½" high.
$70.00 - 85.00

Chicken incubator, pine, label reads "Sure Hatch Incubators, Freemont, Neb., and Indianapolis, Ind." Size: 29¼" wide, 31" deep, 29½" high.
$175.00 - 200.00

At the small town general store where the farmer traded, groceries were available in bulk form to be scooped out of bins, barrels, boxes, or glass containers to meet customer demands. Coffee beans were dipped out of large wooden bins which advertised the company which distributed the product. After the clerk weighed the requested amount, a bit of legerdemain was required to wrap the purchase in paper he tore off from a holder on the counter and tied with string from a metal holder.

Store spool cabinets with drawers sit demurely on dressers to hold jewelry and scarves or they provide a filing space for precious papers. A walnut one with porcelain pulls bears a label which reads:

IMPORTANT

As this CABINET is supplied at a very GREAT EXPENSE
it is respectfully requested that no SPOOL COTTON will
be kept in it except CLARK'S O.N.T. BEST SIX CORD

(O.N.T. stands for "Our New Thread.") Save that label! Clark was proud of its O.N.T. and the container provided so the manufacturer's request is worthy of preservation. At times, spool holders become coffee tables or house hobbies. Display cases, especially those with advertising on them, are sought to show off collections and are collectible in themselves.

Spool cabinet, walnut. Size: 22" wide, 14" deep, 9" high.
$95.00 - 110.00

Coffee bin, pine, label reads "Roth-Homeyer Roasted Coffee." Size: 23" wide, 16" deep, 28" high.
$110.00 - 135.00

Perhaps one corner of the store was the post office where the townspeople could congregate to socialize and collect their mail. Shelves into which letters were flicked for sorting have small compartments which neatly display collections.

Early in this century, drug store soda fountains and candyshops frequently had ice cream tables and chairs where customers sat to sip sodas through a straw or ate sundaes rich with thick sauces. The twisted wire look prevailed and should show signs of wear. If a copper or brass wash was applied, this thin coating should be worn off in spots and not have a new look those made currently have. The heart-back chairs tend to be more sought after than the common variety which loops around to resemble a pair of eye glasses peering at one. Table tops were of marble, wood, or composition material. Booths with their accompanying tables are sought also. Apothecary chests, a frame with multi-drawers, can be functional. Instead of pharmaceutical supplies, homemakers file small sundries inside.

The undertaker, the farmer, the barber, the dentist, the pharmacist, the storekeeper, the blacksmith, the dry goods merchant, the ice man, and others would be surprised if they knew that tools of their trades are home-sweet-home symbols. The carpenter's tote box of yore may be a magazine rack or, when carefully lined, bloom with plants. Tradesmen and professionals of yesteryear might legitimately query, "Has the world gone topsy-turvy?" These take-me-back-to-the-old-days invaders lend individual casual touches to modern homes. They're unsophisticated with a blend of the country in them. They're available for adoption by anyone. They can be primitive and many are mainly plain pine.

Above: Post office sorting box, maple, the A, B, C's are still legible on top of the boxes. Size: 24" wide, 9½" deep, 37" high.

$85.00 - 110.00

Right: Apothecary chest, oak. Size: 28" wide, 11½" deep, 45½" high.
$250.00 - 275.00

136

Gambling stick, used to hang hogs on during butchering time by slitting tendon in leg and hanging one leg over each end of stick. Size: 25″ wide, 8″ high.
$45.00 - 65.00

Cranberry scoop. Size: 37¾″ long.
$85.00 - 100.00

Above: Store coffee bin, pine. Size: 23″ wide, 14″ deep, 32½″ high at back.
$95.00 - 110.00

Left: Grain bin, pine, three compartments. Size: 29¾″ wide, 19¾″ deep, 29½″ high.
$115.00 - 135.00

Hardware store bolt cabinet, oak, 98 drawers. Size: Drawers - 10¼" x 3⅜", 45" high.
$1,350.00

Apothecary chest, pine. Size: 15¾" wide, 11½" deep, 37¼" high.
$450.00 - 475.00

Apothecary chest, pine case, walnut drawer fronts. Size: 76½" wide, 17" deep, 30" high.
$600.00 - 700.

Barbershop stand, oak, circa 1910. Size: 25½" wide, 13½" deep, 37½" high.

$175.00 - 225.00

Shoeshine chair, from old tavern. Size: 37¾" to seat, 53" high.

$175.00 - 200.00

Barber cabinet, pine and poplar. Size: 23½" wide, 11" deep, 22" high.

$75.00 - 90.00

Spool cabinet, walnut. Size: 18½" wide, 15" deep, 7" high. $75.00 - 95.00

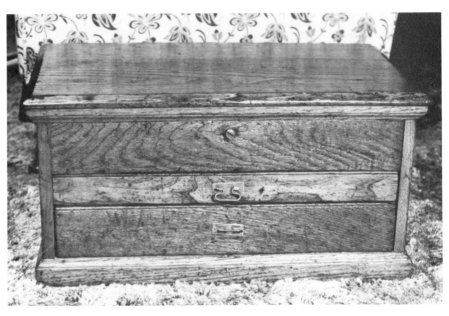

Tool chest, oak, "C. E. Jennings & Co., N.Y." label on inside of front lid. Size: 21" wide, 13" deep, 11" high. $85.00 - 100.00

Carpenter's chest, pine, dovetailed ends. Size: 36" wide, 19" deep, 21" high. $150.00 - 175.00

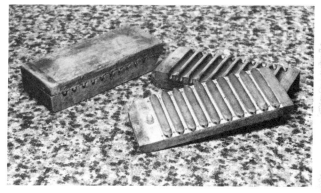

Cranberry barrel. Size: 15¼" wide, 12¼" deep.

$40.00 - 55.00

Handyman's tool box, pine. Size: 13" wide, 8¾" deep, 7½" high.

$50.00 - 65.00

Cigar molds, one closed, one open, makes 10 cigars. Size: 12" wide, 5" deep.

$25.00 - 30.00

Church bench, pine and poplar. Size: 41¼" wide, 17" deep, 33⅓" tall.

$135.00 - 155.00

Other Helpful Books

Aronson, Joseph, *Encyclopedia of Furniture.* Crown Publishers, Inc., New York, N.Y., 1965.

Bradford, Ernie, *Dictionary of Antiques.* The English Universities Press Ltd., London, England, 1963.

Fisher, Leonard Everett, *The Cabinetmaker.* Franklin Watts, Inc., New York, N.Y., 1966.

Horst, Mel and Smith, Elmer L., *Early Country Furniture.* Applied Arts Publishers, Lebanon, Pa., 1970.

Kauffman, Henry J., *Pennsylvania Dutch American Folk Art.* Dover Publications, Inc., New York, N.Y., 1964.

Ormsbee, Thomas H., *The Story of American Furniture.* Pyramid Books, New York, N.Y., 1962.

Rockmore, Cynthia and Julian, *The Room-by-Room Book of American Antiques.* Hawthorne Books, Inc., New York, N.Y., 1970.

Sloane, Eric, *ABC Book of Early Americana.* Doubleday & Company, Inc., Garden City, New York.

Swedberg, Harriett and Robert, *Off Your Rocker, The Art of Repairing and Refinishing Antique Furniture.* Wallace-Homestead Book Company, Des Moines, Iowa, 1976.

Voss, Thomas M., *Antique American Country Furniture.* J.B. Lippincott Company, Philadelphia, Pa., and New York, N.Y., 1978.

Watson, Aldren A., *Country Furniture.* Thomas Y. Crowell Company, New York, N.Y., 1974.

Glossary

Ankle skinner (also carpet cutter; cheese cutter)
Tall rockers, higher than they are wide.

Apothecary chest
Many small drawers in a wooden frame in which a druggist stored pharmaceutical supplies.

Applied
An ornamentation made separately and attached to a piece later.

Apron (also skirt)
A piece used as a structural aid or to hide construction details on chairs, case pieces, and tables. The apron is between the feet at the base of cabinets, cupboards, and chests. On a chair, it is under the seat, and on a table it is beneath the top where the legs connect.

Arrow back
One end of the spindles on a chair or settee resembling arrows.

Bail handle
A metal drawer pull with a half loop pendant fastened to a back plate.

Balloon back
A chair back with a vague resemblance to a round balloon.

Bootjack ends
A foot made by a triangular cutout. Resembles a bootjack used to hold the heel of a boot as the wearer pulled it off.

Boston rocker
A spindle-back rocking chair with a solid wood seat which curves up at the rear and under in front. Usually painted and decorated originally.

Bow-back Windsor
A spindled chair in which a curve in a continuous arch forms the back. The ends are fastened into the wooden seat.

Breadboard ends
Crosswise pieces of wood fastened to the ends of furniture such as a table or chest top or the edges of a door to prevent warping.

Breakfront
Used on some bookcases, desks, wardrobes, and sideboards. The straight lines of the front are broken by a vertical portion which juts out.

Butt joint
The simplest joint. The flat ends of two boards are attached together with no overlap. A drawer side may butt against the front edge.

Cabriole leg
A leg with a double curve which flows out at the knee, in at the ankle, then slightly outward again.

Cane
Long narrow strip of rattan used for weaving chair seats and backs.

Carpet cutter (also ankle skinner; cheese cutter)
Tall rockers, higher than they are wide.

Case piece
A box-like structure such as a cabinet, desk, chest of drawers, or the like.

Chamfer
1) A corner or edge cut off to form a slanting surface.
2) A groove cut in wood.

Cheese cutter (also ankle skinner; carpet cutter)
Tall rockers, higher than they are wide.

Chip carving
A simple carved decoration made with a chisel or gouge.

Circa or c
About; indicates an approximate date, as circa 1900.

Closed cupboard
A cupboard which has doors.

Cobbled
A piece which has had parts added or changed so that it is not in its original condition. Example: a closed cupboard remade into an open pewter cupboard.

Comb-back Windsor
Spindles which resemble a comb in shape, extending above the main part of the back.

Commode
An enclosed cupboard-type washstand.

Cornice
The top horizontal molding on an article of furniture.

Cottage furniture
Factory made, inexpensive furniture produced in the mid- to late-1800s and painted brightly with floral, bird, and similar designs.

Dough box, dough tray, and dough trough
A wooden container in which large amounts of bread dough could be stored to rise. Those with tops could be used as a surface on which to knead the bread and shape the loaves.

Dovetail
Joint made when the triangular projection at the end of one board fits into a triangle cut out of another board much as jigsaw puzzles interlock.

Dowel
A peg or pin which fits into holes in two pieces of wood and holds them together. Old pegs are square.

Drop front
A hinged lid drops down to form a writing surface on a desk.

Dry sink

A cupboard with a well or tray in the top which was usually zinc lined, to be used in the kitchen when water was carried in, not piped into houses.

Escutcheon

A fitting around a keyhole which may be inset or applied.

Extension table

The table top pulls apart so that additional leaves may be added to enlarge it.

Fake

A piece that is created and sold falsely to fool someone or is misrepresented in any way with the intent to defraud.

Fancy chair

Hitchcock chairs and similar ones; almost any painted and decorated chair.

Fall front

A hinged lid on a desk which drops down to form a writing surface.

Finger grip

A groove cut in lower front edge of a drawer to use in place of a knob or handle.

Finial

A carved, turned, or cast terminal decoration on a piece; for example, cannonball finials on a bed post.

Flush

Level with the surrounding surface.

Gateleg

A swinging leg with a stretcher to serve as a support for a drop leaf on a table.

Geometric

A design made with interlacing circles, squares, triangles, or similar designs.

Graining

Paint applied to represent the grain of a specific wood.

Half spindle

The spindles on a chair back go up midway to fit into a slat rather than extending from the seat to the top rail.

Hardware

Metal nails, screws, straps, hinges, escutcheons, and the like on a piece. Pulls and handles are called "hardware" even when they are not metal but are ceramic, glass, ivory, etc.

Hitchcock

In the 1820-1850s Lambert Hitchcock made painted and decorated chairs similar to Sheraton fancy chairs. Other companies made them also, but they are generally called Hitchcock chairs.

Hood

An arched top covering.

Incised

Design cut or engraved into the surface.

Joiner

An old-time craftsman who did not use metal or glue to hold pieces together. Wooden pegs, dovetails, mortise and tenons, etc. attached parts to each other in furniture making.

Kerf Marks

The marks left by a saw. Normally, before the 1850s, a straight blade was used and made up and down parallel rows. The circular saw leaves almost semi-circular rows and first appeared in the United States about 1820, but probably was not used generally until the 1850s.

Lap or rabbet joint

Boards cut so that a right angle in the front of one slips into a right angle cut in the back of another to fit smoothly.

Lathe

A machine for shaping wood by holding it against a cutting tool. Turned legs for tables and chairs are made on a lathe.

Marriage

Pieces of furniture joined as one when they were not originally meant to go together. Example: a bookcase top is added to a drop front desk to form a secretary.

Milk paint

Paint with a milk base with pigment and other ingredients added. Made at home in the 1800s. Commonly red, blue, gray.

Miter joint

The ends of two boards are cut at a slant so they can be matched together to form a right angle and pegged to stay in position. Example: rectangular or square picture frames are usually joined in this manner.

Molding

A continuous decorative edging carved in or applied to furniture.

Mortise and tenon

The mortise is a slot or hole in a piece of wood. A tenon is a protruding tongue or prong in another piece of wood which fits snugly into the mortise to form a strong joint. They may be pegged where they join.

Open cupboard

One with no doors.

Ogee

A molding with a double continuous curve.

Panel

A square or rectangular board set into a grooved framework. A flush panel is level with its frame. A sunken panel is beneath it, while a raised panel rises above the surrounding surface.

Pegged

Instead of nails or screws, a wooden pin or dowel (peg) holds two pieces of board together at a joint. Old pegs appear square rather than round.

Pewter cupboard
An open cupboard (without doors). Supposedly, pewter, an alloy of mainly copper and tin, was displayed in it.

Pie safe
A closed cupboard with pierced tin panels said to deter rodents and flies who might eat the baked goods inside. Screening or punched board panels may also be used.

Pierced tin
Pieces of tin perforated in patterns. The holes could be pierced either in or out. See pie safe, above.

Pillow rail
Often found on Hitchcock chairs. An elliptical section on the top rail.

Plank seat
A seat formed from one piece of wood.

Rabbet or lap joint
Boards cut so that a right angle in the front of one slips into a right angle cut in the back of another to fit smoothly.

Rattan
A climbing palm with long slender tough stems which are used for cane and wicker work.

Reproduction (repro)
A copy or imitation. Reproductions are fraudulent only when they are made with the intent to deceive and are sold as the genuine article.

Rose cap
A Norwegian cupboard-desk combination.

Rung (also stretcher; runner)
A runner or cross piece which connects cabinet, chair, or table legs at the bottom. Sometimes called a stretcher.

Runner
1) Another name for the rocker on a rocking chair.
2) Slides which support desk drop lids.
3) A guide strip to support a drawer.
4) A rung or stretcher.

Rush
A marsh plant used to make woven chair seats. Today a rolled paper is usually used.

Scalloped
A series of curves in an ornamental edge patterned after the shape of a shell.

Scribe line
The mark left by a sharp instrument which cuts a shallow, narrow groove to show where and how two parts of a piece of furniture should be joined.

Settee
A light, open, low-back seat about double the width of a chair.

Settle
An all wooden, high-back settee with solid sides which protect the sitters from drafts.

Shaker
A religious community where plain, yet attractive, strong furniture was designed and sold to the public. Shaker chairs have a fragile appearance but are durable. Slat-backs (ladder-backs) with woven seats were marketed.

Skirt (also apron)
Frequently used as a decorative means to hide the construction of a piece, such as where the legs are attached to the top of a table. Appears beneath the seat on chairs or near the base on cupboards, chests, and cabinets.

Slant front
The hinged drop lid on a desk or secretary which provides a writing surface when it is opened and slants back when closed.

Slat
Horizontal crossbar in chair backs.

Spindle
A slender rod, often in a chair back, as in the Windsor chairs.

Splat
The center upright in a chair back which can be plain or decorative.

Splay
Slant out, especially chair legs which slant out from the seat to the floor.

Spool turning
Resembles spools, knobs, balls, or similar objects strung together in a row. Spindles and table legs may have spool turnings.

Stile
The vertical piece in a frame or panel in furniture.

Stretchers (also rung; runner)
The crosspieces or rungs which connect table, cabinet, or chair legs.

Tape
Strips of colored fabric used by Shakers to weave chair seats.

Tenon
A tongue or prong which fits tightly into a mortise (slot or hole) to join together two furniture parts. May be pegged.

Tongue and groove
When a continuous tongue sticks out at the end of a board and is inserted into a corresponding groove cut into the wooden piece with which it is to be joined.

Turning
Shaping wood on a lathe with chisels to form table and chair legs, and other turned pieces.

Windsor chair
American Windsors have backs with many slender spindles and legs which are inserted into the seat without being framed by aprons (skirts).

Wing
Solid sides which project out from the back of a chair to protect a sitter from drafts.

Index

A

Age, ways of detecting, 17-30
    glass, 22, 28-29
    hardware, 19-21
    joints, 23-26
    paint, 22-23
    patina, 18
    pegs, 19
    shrinkage, 28
    smell, 30
    styles, 30
    thickness, wood, 28
    tools, 26
    wear, 18
Alterations, how to detect, 16-17
Antique marriages, 13, 17, 66
    defined, 13-14

B

Baby furniture, 125-132
Banquet board, 84
Bath tub, 33
Bedchamber furniture, 110-124, 127-128
    Bedroom, or cottage suite, 112-114
    Beds, 110-111, 127-128
        cannonball, 110
        children's, 127-128
        Jenny Lind, 110-111
        rope, 73, 77, 110
        spool, 110-111, 127
        trundle, 111
    Closet and armoires, 114
    Desks, 114-116
    Dressers and chests, 112, 114, 129
Bedroom suite, 112-114
Beds, 110-111, 127-128
Benches, 81-83
    Deacon's, 94
    "Mammy," 82
    settle, 82-83
    water, 37
Boston rocker, 88-89
    children's, 126
Butt joint, 25

C

Cabinet
    Hoosier, 56
    kitchen, 56
Cannonball bed, 73, 110
Chair, 85-90, 92, 100-109, 125-126
    children's, 125-126, 131-132
    Hitchcock, 9, 90, 102
    "knocked down," 90
    ladder back, 92, 100-101
    rocker, 87, 88-89, 108-109, 125-126
        Boston, 88-89
        Lincoln, 89
    seats, 92
    Windsor, 85-88, 105-108, 131
        firehouse, 87-88, 107
        rocking, 87
        Rod-back, 87, 103, 105-106
        writing, 87
Chests
    children's, 128
    clothes, 114
    hope or dowry, 112
    meal, grain, or flour, 51, 69, 70
Children's furniture, 73, 74, 77, 125-132
Closets and armoires, 114
Cobbled, defined, 13, 14-15
Commodes, 34, 35, 40, 44, 45
Cottage suite, 9, 112-114
Country furniture, defined, 6, 9, 12
Cradle, 127-128
    doll, 130
Cupboard, pewter, 54, 57-68

D

Desks, 8, 11, 17, 78-80, 119-121
    children's, 126-127
Dough, bread, containers for, 47-49, 78
Dovetail joints, 25-26
Draw table, 85
Dresser
    clothes, 114
    kitchen, 54
    Welsh, 54
Dry sink, 17, 36-37, 40-43

F

Fakes, 15
Farm primitives, 95, 134, 137, 141
Firehouse Windsor chair, 87-88
Funeral articles, 133

G

Gate leg table, 84
General-store primitives, 135-137
Glass, 22, 28-29, 55
    in detecting age, 28-29
Graining, 21, 22, 90, 112

H

Hardware, 17
    in detecting age, 19-21
Harvest table, 84
Hitchcock chair, 9, 90, 102
Hoosier cabinet, 56, 76
Hope chest, 112

J

Jenny Lind bed, 110-111
Joiner, 23-24
Joint
    defined, 24-26
    in detecting age, 23-26

K

Kitchen cabinet, 56
Kitchen primitive, 134
Kitchen utensils, 51-52
"Knocked down" chairs, 90

L

Ladder-back chair, 92, 100-101
Lap joint, 25
Lincoln rocker, 89

M

"Mammy" bench, 82
Milk paint, recipe for, 23
Miter joint, 25
Mortise and tenon, 24

O

Outhouse, 32

P

Paint
    in detecting age, 22-23
    graining, 21, 22, 112
    milk paint, recipe for, 23
Patina, defined, 18
Pennsylvania Dutch, 102, 112
Pie safe, 50-51, 64
Pewter cupboard, 54
Plumbing furnishings, 31-45
    bath tub, 33
    commode, 34
    dry sink, 36-37
    pump, 31-32
    toilet article, 33-34
    washer, clothes, 37-39
    washstand, 34-35, 40, 44-45, 116-117
Prices, 6
    determination of, 6
Primitives, 133-136
    defined, 6, 9-12
    farm, 134
    funeral, 133
    general-store, 135-136
    kitchen, 134
    various professions, 136
Pump, 31-32

R

Rabbet joint, 25
"Receet" for washing clothes, 38
Refectory table, 74, 85
Reproductions, 15
Rocking chairs, 87, 88-89, 108-109, 125-126
    children's, 125-126
    Boston, 88-89
    Lincoln, 89
    Windsor, 87
Rodback Windsor chair, 37, 87, 103, 105-106
Rope bed, 73, 77, 110

S

Salesmen's samples, 128-129
Seats, chair, materials, 92, 102, 109, 125, 132
Settle bench, 82
Settle table, 82-83, 96
Shaker furniture, 27, 91-92, 102, 109

Shrinkage, in detecting age, 28
Smell, in detecting age, 30
Spool bed, 110-111, 127
Styles, in detecting age, 30

T
Tables, 82-85, 126
    banquet board, 84
    children's, 126
    draw, 85
    gate leg, 84
    harvest, 84
    refectory, 74, 85
    settle, 82-83, 96
    trestle, 84
Thickness, wood, in detecting age, 28
Toilet, defined, 20, 31
Toilet article, 33-34
Tongue and groove, 25
Tools, in detecting age, 26
Toys, 128-130
Treenware, 52-53
Trestle table, 84
Trundle bed, 111
Trunks, 120-124

W
Washer, clothes, 37-39
Washstand, 34-35, 40, 44-45, 116-117
Water bench, 37
Wear, signs of, in detecting age, 18-19
Wedge, 25
Welsh dresser, 54
Windsor chair, 85-88, 105-108, 131
    captain's, 88
    children's, 126, 131
    firehouse, 87-88, 107
    rocking, 87
    Rod-back, 87, 103, 105-106
    writing, 87

About the Authors

Bob and Harriett Swedberg enjoy antiques and especially like the friendships made through two decades of collecting. Authors of two other antique books include *Off Your Rocker,* which tells how to refinish woods, care for metals, etc. and *Victorian Furniture Styles and Prices,* a most successful work.

The Swedbergs conduct seminars at universities, teach classes, lecture, write for periodicals and exhibit at antique shows frequently. They are interested in historical preservation and serve on the Colonel (George) Davenport Historical Foundation Board.

Bob, an English teacher, did his undergraduate study at North Park College, Chicago, and Northwestern University and received his masters from the University of Iowa. Harriett graduated from Hanover College, Indiana, and continued her studies at McCormick Theological Seminary's Presbyterian College. They reside in Moline, Illinois and are continally seeking to increase their knowledge about antiques.